COOK
for the
SOUL

LUCY LORD

COOK
for the
SOUL

Over 80 fresh, fun and creative
recipes to feed your soul

'Enjoy the cake.
Be selfish with
your sleep. Move,
often. Be kind
with your words.
Be generous
with your actions.'

INTRODUCTION

Much like in life, for me the biggest satisfaction in the kitchen comes from choosing to step outside my comfort zone, learning to 'fail forward', becoming more adaptable and then sharing my learnings with others so that they can experience the joy in creating these dishes themselves.

Once I became more confident in the kitchen and had built up a small handful of recipes that I loved and made regularly, I began to stretch myself with new skills and more challenging recipes. I found that the greatest satisfaction wasn't just learning the new skill, but sharing it – and the creations that came from it – with others. There is no better compliment than somebody trying a bake you've brought in to work or leaving after a dinner you've prepared and asking for the recipe! Dinner parties, picnics, brunches, barbecues, celebrations and birthdays – I began to see any gathering, large or small, as an excuse to get creative, to bring a new dish or homemade drinks mix or to bake a cake to share my passion and love. Life is about living, enjoying and connecting – and food is just one of the many ways to do that.

If you're used to just cooking for yourself, it can be quite overwhelming when there's more than a few pots and pans on the go, so in this book I've worked hard to build on the foundations of *Food for the Soul*'s philosophy of keeping recipes simple but special, approachable and accessible to all. You'll find tips, tricks and hacks for better organisation, kitchen efficiency and how to really make the most of everything, from ingredients to time. From creating a capsule storecupboard (see page 13) so you always have delicious recipes to fall back on, to utilising the fridge and freezer so that when you make recipes designed to share (such as the lasagne on page 84), you can keep any extras and leftovers. Learn how to transform leftovers into a whole new dish or tuck into extras yourself to enjoy all over again – minus prep time and washing up!

More than just the food we eat, I want to help improve our whole experience of food, from buying it to how best to store it, cooking it, sitting down to enjoy it and making use of leftovers. Along with easy swaps or ingredient alternatives, the notes include information on which recipes are great to make ahead, how and when you can refrigerate or freeze them, so that even for last-minute dinner decisions, you'll always have something delicious ready to go, whether just for yourself or to share.

I hope you can use these recipes to reconnect with food, with the people around you and – more importantly – with yourself, inside and outside of the kitchen.

KEY TO SYMBOLS

- **V** vegetarian
- **VE** vegan
- **DF** dairy free
- **GF** gluten free
- **❄** good for freezing

Your kitchen space

Our environment is everything. From the people we surround ourselves with, whether in person or online, to our office spaces and how efficiently we work in them, to our bedrooms and how well we sleep. The joy of making a delicious dish is easily dampened if you don't feel at ease while making it or have a mountain of unnecessary dishes to wash up after. You can love your job but if you hate your office environment it can impact everything – the kitchen is no different! It may be the heart of the home for some, but for others it's a place of uncertainty, dread and fear.

Here are some of my top tips to make the most of the space you have. These tips have helped me keep a smooth-running kitchen, no matter how big or small. I started my website cooking in a tiny, postage-stamp-sized kitchen in a shared flat on Bondi beach with one fridge shelf; since then I've lived, house-sat and worked from small hotel rooms, studio apartments, beachfront manors and grand country mansions. What I've come to respect is it's not the space we have, it's how we use that space that makes the difference.

1. Read the recipe through first. I know, it sounds obvious, but it gives you a good overview of what's expected and prevents an unexpected 'marinate overnight' step when you're looking to have something on the table within the hour.

2. Pull out all of the equipment and ingredients you'll need first. This stops you from going back and forth from cupboards to fridges, preventing sticky door handles, and it avoids stress and the likelihood of something burning as you're looking for that spatula.

3. I set out separate rubbish/recycling/compost bowls on the counter so that once I'm finished cooking, these can go straight in their respective bins and there's less back-and-forth.

4. Use mugs for 'dry' and 'wet' utensils. This stops sauce drips and the need for reaching for a clean spoon every time you need to measure 1 teaspoon of something.

5. Clean up along the way – in those spaces of time when something is in the oven, simmering or left to cool, resist scrolling on your phone and start clearing up. There's no better feeling than finishing a meal and being able to relax, knowing that there's little or no washing up to do.

6. Personal touches. When you're spending more time in your kitchen, adding personal touches and treats will make a real difference to how you appreciate your space – think lovely hand soap or candles, framed photos of travels or loved ones, house plants or your favourite cookery books. These help create a space you'll look forward to spending time in.

7. Music! Perhaps my favourite tip: I have background music on nearly all hours of the day, but if I could keep it for just one thing, it would be creating food. Science has shown that music can help create a calming environment, lessen anxiety, reduce stress and support a creative flow state. I use Spotify to create playlists to put on shuffle and get lost in.

Utensils

You don't need lots of equipment for the kitchen or even anything particularly fancy. I waited 10 years before I bought my first stand mixer, and unless you're baking a lot or for many mouths, they're really not a necessity. Here are a few things I couldn't live without:

1. **Silicone spatulas. I mostly use these for baking – they get every scrap of dough, sauce or buttercream from the bowl.**

2. **Pots and pans. Buy a good-quality set and you'll be set up for years. As a foundation, I'd recommend a small and large frying pan, a small and large saucepan and a large, deep stock pot.**

3. **Hand-held stick blender. I bought one relatively cheaply that has multi-head attachments (whisk, blender, small food processor) and it's brilliant for making pesto, grinding seeds and spices, blending soups and whisking egg whites.**

Eating

Just as important as the space we create in, the space we eat in matters too. Although life can get in the way sometimes and we can't always lay the table just for ourselves, making the effort when we can really does make a difference. Studies show that eating food while sitting down aids digestion and reduces any tendencies to overeat; meanwhile, distracted eating (while scrolling our phones, sitting at a desk, walking or driving) all increase these tendencies. Even if you're sat by yourself on a park bench, get comfortable and make the time for yourself to really enjoy what you're eating. And whether you have friends over or it's just you, think about lighting a candle and putting some good background music on, as these can really help you to further enjoy your experience.

If you regularly eat meals on the go, try stopping to sit down and eat whenever you can. Make a note of whether you felt any better or noticed any differences during or after. Often, the best person to listen to for advice is ourselves.

Storage

Before going out and buying any new ingredients, do a stock-check of what you already have in your fridge, freezer and storecupboard. Make a note on your phone or calendar to do this regularly; it makes it so much easier to keep on top of and helps with everything from reducing waste to finding the ingredient you were looking for in the first place. Spending a little time one weekend morning to organise what you have already will help you throughout the week to 'glance' at cupboards, stop over-buying and become more efficient with your time and money.

1. **Check sell-by dates, especially on those things you don't use often or much of, like spices, baking powder and tinned goods.**

2. **Group similar foods together so you can see what you have at a glance: flours, sugars, tinned savoury, tinned sweet.**

3. **Label foods in your freezer with what they are and the date they were frozen.**

4. For cooked food going back into the fridge or freezer, leave to cool completely and keep in an airtight container. Wrap any solid foods (such as cakes) going into the freezer tightly in cling film and then in an airtight container to prevent freezer burn.

5. I don't think it's necessary to buy lots of storage containers for every individual type of nut and seed, but if you have lots of loose items, large see-through storage boxes are a cheap and effective way of keeping similar things tidy. Recycled glass jars are great for storage too.

6. Lots of food packets now come with built-in self-sticking seals; otherwise, a handful of food clips are great at keeping food fresh and avoiding crumb spillages, drying out and mould.

7. Have a small, magnetic fridge shopping list (or pin one inside a storage cupboard) or keep a list on your notes app, to make a note of anything running low to buy on your next food shop.

'The key to success is to start before you're ready.'

Creating a capsule food cupboard

Despite loving my time in the kitchen, I rarely have time to cook every meal from scratch. I like to batch-cook a handful of recipes every few weeks and stash them in the freezer so I always have a few quick, homemade meals to hand. It is one of my greatest life (and time) hacks. Throughout this book I've indicated which recipes are suitable for freezing. I also like to rotate a handful of seasonal recipes that I can whip up in 20 minutes or fewer and I'll keep ingredients for these in my capsule cupboard (see the Quick & Simple chapter on page 52).

Everyone's capsule food cupboard will differ but here are a few staples with a longer shelf life that I am always grateful to have:

1. Spices – my favourites are ground cinnamon, cumin and coriander and dried oregano, rosemary and thyme.

2. Tinned tomatoes, coconut milk, chickpeas, butter beans and – of course – baked beans.

3. Pouches of lentils and rice, especially the flavoured ones. These are great if you're cooking for one or two to add a bit of flavour variety to meals that you cook regularly.

4. Nut butters, tahini, honey, maple syrup, good-quality balsamic vinegar and olive oil. I'll often throw together a rogue salad dressing with these and it completely lifts a salad or vegetables.

5. Onions, garlic, sweet potatoes, white potatoes. Root vegetables have a great shelf life and last a lot longer than fruits or leafy greens.

BREAKFASTS & BRUNCHES

BREAKFASTS & BRUNCHES

Whether you're making breakfast or brunch – for yourself or for several mouths to feed – it's usually a meal we don't associate with creativity or variety. With a lack of time, lack of sleep, we tend to reach for something to tick a box and very rarely spend time savouring it or using it as a way to set the pace for the day, as maybe we should.

The breakfast and brunch scene has exploded in recent years with more people making plans to catch up over a coffee and have a bite to eat in the morning rather than a late-night meal and cocktails. I love both, but there's something special about the magic of mornings: they're full of possibility for the day ahead, new beginnings and an opportunity to connect with ourselves and those around us.

It can be hard to please everyone, but making a simple breakfast station set up at the table is a great way to capture lots of flavours and options without going to lots of extra time, preparation or work. 'Four ways' toast toppers and porridges are ideal for this, with something for everyone, and toppings can even be prepared the day before if you have people over for breakfast before a day out. Other breakfast dishes such as the Menemen (Turkish scrambled eggs), green shakshuka or overnight French toast tray can be made in one large dish and

'If you are more fortunate than others, build a longer table, not a taller fence.'

plonked in the middle of the dining table, with toast to dip and dunk or berries and sauces for sweet dishes so everyone can help themselves. I love eating in this way, it brings a real sense of community and sharing to the table, even if there's just two of you.

Of course, we can't always carve out the time to have a slower-paced start to the morning, especially during the working week. Many of my favourite morning starts have also involved rushing to get out the door, to the beach or in the car to chase a sunrise, have a swim, hit the gym or begin a morning hike. For these occasions, I love bringing breakfast with me and whoever else might join, such as the no-bake date and tahini bars or the American blueberry muffins. Easily transportable, no fridge required and they always trump the shop-bought versions (that's if shops are even open or close by, which often they're not).

Menemen – Turkish scrambled eggs
Porridge 4 ways
No-bake date and tahini granola bars
Bakery-style American blueberry muffins
Toast toppers 4 ways
Sweetcorn fritters with feta, chilli and lime
Green shakshuka
Overnight French toast tray

Menemen – Turkish scrambled eggs

SERVES 4 | **TIME TO MAKE** 20 MINS | **SUITABLE FOR** V GF

A beautiful and speedy dish, menemen is simple enough to be pulled together in fewer than 20 minutes; and cooked in one large pan, it makes for minimal washing up too. A soft egg scramble with silky green and red peppers, tomato and loaded with herbs and spices, serve with toasted sourdough or flatbreads to dip in and soak up the delicious sauce.

2 tbsp olive oil
1 pointed red pepper, diced
1 green pepper, diced
2 garlic cloves, crushed
1 tbsp tomato purée
227g tin chopped tomatoes
½ tsp paprika
1 tsp chilli flakes
1 tsp salt, plus more to taste
6 large eggs
1 tbsp chopped parsley
80g crumbled feta, to serve
Freshly ground black pepper
Toast or warm flatbreads, to serve

1. Heat the olive oil in a large, frying pan over a medium heat, then add the peppers and sauté for a few minutes until they start to soften. Add the garlic and tomato purée and sauté for another minute until aromatic.

2. Pour in the chopped tomatoes, paprika, chilli flakes and salt, stir to mix, then let it simmer for 5 minutes to reduce the liquid.

3. Break the eggs into a small bowl and whisk with a fork. Once the tomato sauce has reduced and thickened, pour the eggs over and use a wooden spoon to gently stir them into the mixture, working from the outside in. Reduce the heat to low–medium and continue to cook, uncovered, for a few minutes while the eggs cook, stirring often.

4. Remove from the heat just before the eggs have set (they will continue to cook off the heat). Taste to season for salt, then finish with the chopped parsley and crumbled feta and lots of freshly ground black pepper. Serve with toast or flatbreads.

Notes
· I find tomato-based dishes always need a little bit more salt than other dishes, so make sure you taste as you go and build up the salt in layers rather than throw it all in at the end. You can always add more but you can't take it out once it's in!
· To make this gluten free, serve with gluten-free bread.

Porridge 4 ways

SERVES	TIME TO MAKE	SUITABLE FOR
6	15 MINS	GF

FOR THE PORRIDGE
240g rolled oats (see Notes)
360ml milk
1 tsp salt

For cooler mornings, porridge is an easy, comforting and quick option but so often gets painted as bland, boring and tasteless. This is where the topping stations really come in! Porridge cooked over the stove takes a few minutes more than being pinged in a microwave, but really does result in a much creamier base. With friends, I love serving one giant bowl of porridge with several options for toppings, similar to hotel and buffet breakfast stations – it can transform one dish into three or more and has something to suit everyone. Much more exciting than the generic handful of blueberries and honey.

1. Put the oats in a small saucepan, add the milk and 360ml water and allow to sit for 5–10 minutes (while you prepare the toppings).

2. Place the saucepan over a medium heat, add the salt and bring to a gentle simmer

3. Simmer for about 5 minutes until creamy, gently stirring constantly. Add a splash more liquid if needed.

Notes
· Look for Scottish oats for a smoother, creamier texture – these take about 10 minutes to cook. Rolled oats, jumbo oats or old-fashioned oats have a larger surface area so take 5–6 minutes but still have a creamy, slightly chewier texture. Avoid instant or quick oats in this dish as these are far too small and powdery.
· I like using a 50:50 mix of milk and water; I think this creates the best creamy consistency without being too heavy.
· You can use any type of milk alternative to make this dairy free.
· Use certified 'gluten-free' oats if you need these to be GF.

APRICOT, MAPLE SYRUP AND WALNUT

SERVES **2** | SUITABLE FOR

30g dried apricots
20g walnuts, roughly chopped
2 tbsp maple syrup
2 tsp fresh thyme leaves

1. Put the dried apricots into a bowl and pour over just enough boiling water to cover them. Leave for at least 10 minutes – this will help plump them up. Drain, discard the liquid and cut in half widthways (so they still look whole).

2. Pile the apricots on top of the porridge, along with the chopped walnuts, maple syrup and a sprinkle of thyme leaves.

BLACKBERRIES, HONEY AND THYME

SERVES **2** | SUITABLE FOR

30g fresh blackberries
20g flaked almonds
2 tbsp honey
2 tsp fresh thyme leaves

1. Top the porridge with the blackberries and flaked almonds, then drizzle over the honey and sprinkle with thyme leaves.

APRICOT, COCONUT AND LIME

SERVES **2** | SUITABLE FOR

Zest of 1 lime
1 tbsp soft dark brown sugar
30g toasted coconut flakes
2 tbsp almond butter

1. Combine the lime zest, brown sugar and toasted coconut flakes in a small bowl.

2. Stir the almond butter through the porridge bowls, then top with the zest and coconut mix.

BANANA, TAHINI AND SESAME SEEDS

SERVES **2** | SUITABLE FOR

1 tbsp soft dark brown sugar
1 tbsp sesame seeds
Pinch of ground cinnamon
2 tbsp tahini
1 banana, peeled and chopped into coins

1. In a small bowl, combine the brown sugar, sesame seeds and cinnamon.

2. Stir the tahini through the porridge bowls and sprinkle over the sesame mix and the banana pieces.

No-bake date and tahini granola bars

MAKES	HANDS-ON	HANDS-OFF	SUITABLE FOR
8	30 MINS	2 HRS	VE GF ❄

60g pecans
120g Medjool dates, pitted
120g rolled oats
80g flaked almonds
30g sesame seeds (I use black)
1 tsp sea salt
120g hulled tahini (see Notes)
8 tbsp rice malt syrup
4 tbsp coconut oil
1 tsp vanilla bean paste (or use
   vanilla extract)
60g dark chocolate chips

Notes
*· Hulled tahini is made with sesame
  seeds with their outer coating
  removed; they have a less bitter
  taste but regular tahini works just
  as well.*
*· Swap the rice malt syrup for honey
  or golden syrup.*
*· Swap the specified nuts, seeds
  and dried fruits for your favourite
  variations – just keep the weight
  ratios and roughly chop larger
  ingredients.*
*· Use your favourite nut butter instead
  of tahini.*
*· Use certified 'gluten-free' oats if you
  need these to be GF.*
*· Will keep for 3 days or once cooled,
  keep in the fridge for up to 5 days or
  freeze for up to 3 months.*

Quick, easy and so much more delicious than those you'd buy from a supermarket! Mix them up by swapping in your favourite flavour combinations, ingredients or whatever you have to use up in your cupboard (see Notes). Eat them as they are or crumble over yoghurts and smoothies. Fridge- and freezer-friendly, these will be one of your new go-to recipes! I love having a stash in my freezer for last-minute 'let's catch a sunrise' plans or days I know I'm going to be pushed for time.

1. Preheat the oven to 220°C/200°C fan and line a 20cm square baking tin with baking paper and set aside.

2. Use a sharp knife to roughly chop the pecans and Medjool dates.

3. In a large bowl, mix the oats, flaked almonds, chopped pecans and dates, sesame seeds and salt together.

4. Melt the tahini, rice malt syrup and coconut oil together in a large saucepan over a low–medium heat until smooth. Remove from the heat, add the vanilla and pour the dry ingredients into the saucepan. Use a spatula or spoon to mix everything together until evenly coated.

5. Add the chocolate chips and mix through again. Pour the mixture into the prepared baking tin and use a spatula or the back of a spoon to spread the mixture evenly, pressing down firmly to compact everything together.

6. Chill in the fridge for at least 2 hours.

Bakery-style American blueberry muffins

MAKES | TIME TO MAKE | SUITABLE FOR
12 LARGE **30** MINS

It's hard to beat proper bakery-style muffins – the small, sickly and sticky supermarket ones that only have a few blueberries dotted through rarely live up to expectations. I love (and will happily queue) for a high-domed, crunchy-topped muffin, studded evenly with blueberries throughout. But recreating this at home can come with its challenges: sinking blueberries, green- or blue-streaked batter, flat muffin tops. This is one recipe where understanding the science of baking really does come into play.

380g plain flour
3 tsp baking powder
½ tsp bicarbonate of soda
½ tsp salt
200g caster sugar
250ml buttermilk
80g butter, melted and slightly cooled
4 tbsp vegetable oil
2 large eggs
2 tsp vanilla bean paste (or use vanilla extract)
200g blueberries
3 tbsp demerara sugar, for sprinkling

Notes
- *The raising agents start to work as soon as the wet ingredients hit the batter, so work quickly to mix and get the muffins into the oven.*
- *Starting the oven at a high temperature creates a higher 'dome' on the muffins. Remember to reduce the temperature though!*
- *Once cooled, will keep for 3 days or wrap tightly in cling film and freeze in an airtight container for up to 3 months.*

1. Preheat the oven to 230°C/210°C fan and line a muffin tin with paper liners.

2. Sift the flour, baking powder, bicarbonate of soda and salt together in a large bowl. Add the sugar and stir everything together well.

3. Add the buttermilk, melted butter, oil, eggs and vanilla to a measuring jug and whisk together with a fork.

4. Make a well in the flour bowl and pour in the wet ingredients. Gently fold until just combined, being careful not to overmix – the batter will be thick and heavy. Use a spoon to pile 1 tablespoon of the batter into the bottom of each case.

5. Add the blueberries to the remaining batter in the bowl and gently fold once or twice to mix. Spoon this batter into the cases, filling to the top. Sprinkle over the demerara sugar and then slide them into the oven. Bake for 5 minutes, then reduce the temperature to 200°C/180°C fan and bake for another 12–15 minutes until golden, risen and a clean skewer inserted in the centre comes out with no wet batter streaks.

6. Remove from the oven and leave until just cool enough to touch before popping the muffins out of the tin and transferring to a wire rack to cool.

Toast toppers 4 ways

TIME TO MAKE

🕐 **10** MINS

Good-quality bread, sliced for the toast

Similar to the porridge on page 20, this is an easy way to cater for a crowd by keeping one staple base (here, it's the toast) and providing smaller plates or bowls with various options for people to mix and match as they like.

AVOCADO, FETA & CHILLI

SERVES **2** | SUITABLE FOR **V**

1 avocado, peeled, stoned and roughly chopped
40g feta, crumbled
Pinch of chilli flakes
Pinch of sea salt
Fresh herbs (I like basil and dill)

In a small bowl, use a fork to mash the avocado and feta together. Spread this mixture across the toast then finish with chilli flakes, salt and fresh herbs.

ALMOND BUTTER, RASPBERRIES & COCONUT

SERVES **2** | SUITABLE FOR **VE**

2 tbsp almond butter
30g fresh raspberries
20g toasted coconut flakes
Pinch of ground cinnamon

Spread the almond butter over the toast, top with the raspberries and use the back of a fork to roughly mash them into the toast. Top with the toasted coconut flakes and a pinch of cinnamon.

FIG, RICOTTA & THYME

SERVES **2** | SUITABLE FOR **V**

2 tbsp ricotta
2 fresh figs, sliced
1 tbsp honey
1 tsp fresh thyme leaves

Spread the ricotta over the toast, then top with the fresh figs, honey and a sprinkle of thyme leaves.

GARLIC, TOMATO, OLIVE OIL & BASIL

SERVES **2** | SUITABLE FOR **VE**

1 garlic clove, halved
2 tomatoes, finely sliced
1 tbsp olive oil
Fresh basil
Pinch of salt
Fresh ground black pepper

While the toast is still warm, rub the garlic all over it. Top with sliced tomatoes, drizzle of olive oil, salt and freshly ground pepper, then basil to finish.

Sweetcorn fritters with feta, chilli and lime

SERVES | TIME TO MAKE | SUITABLE FOR
4 | 25 MINS | ❄ Ⓥ

If I go out for breakfast, I'll usually look for a sweetcorn fritter dish on the menu – they are so delicious and usually come with a variety of toppings. These are bursting with sweetcorn kernels, salty feta and a bit of spice from the chilli. Loaded with fresh herbs, I like to make extra and then warm them up in the toaster or under the grill for the next few mornings.

200g plain flour
1 tsp baking powder
2 large eggs
8 tbsp milk
600g sweetcorn kernels
120g feta
4 spring onions, trimmed and
    finely chopped
2 red chillies, deseeded and finely
    chopped
2 tbsp finely chopped coriander
    and/or chives
2 tbsp olive oil
Salt and freshly ground black
    pepper

TO SERVE
Lime wedges, sliced avocado,
    smoked salmon, crispy bacon,
    poached eggs or sour cream
    and lots of fresh herbs

1. Mix the flour and baking powder together in a large bowl.

2. Whisk the eggs and milk together in a jug with some salt and pepper, then add to the bowl of flour and stir until a paste forms. Fold in the sweetcorn, feta, spring onions, chillies and fresh herbs.

3. Heat 1 tablespoon of olive oil in a large non-stick pan over a medium–high heat and use a ladle or tablespoon to measure out about 2 heaped tablespoons of batter per fritter, cooking them 2 or 3 at a time.

4. Cook the fritters for about 2 minutes on each side, or until puffed up, golden and crispy. Flip them to cook on the other side.

5. Keep the cooked fritters warm in a low oven while you cook the remaining ones, adding more oil to the pan as needed. Grind over some black pepper and serve with your choice of toppings.

Note
· Store in an airtight container in the fridge for up to 3 days.

Green shakshuka

SERVES | TIME TO MAKE | SUITABLE FOR

4 | ⏱ 25 MINS | Ⓥ GF

One of my favourite spots for breakfast in North Bondi is Israeli café Shuk. Tucked away from the beach front, it occupies a quiet corner of Bondi but from sunrise until sunset it's hustling, bustling and always busy. It was here that I first saw green shaksuka on a menu (it's usually baked in a rich, red, tomato-based sauce) and I fell in love instantly. A lighter, brighter version of the popular breakfast dish, here eggs are baked among leeks, onions, dark leafy greens, sweet peas and salty olives and feta. Serve with a squeeze of lemon to lift the flavours and, of course, fresh herbs and toasted bread to dip into the yolks.

1 tsp fennel seeds
1 tsp cumin seeds
2 tbsp olive oil
1 onion, diced
1 leek, trimmed and diced
3 garlic cloves, finely chopped
80g frozen peas
60g kale or Swiss chard, chopped
Vegetable stock cube, dissolved
    in 150ml water
60g spinach
4 large eggs
120g feta, crumbled
60g black pitted olives, roughly
    chopped
Salt and freshly ground black
    pepper
Lemon wedges, dill, parsley
    and chilli flakes (optional),
    to garnish
Toasted bread, to serve

1. Tip the fennel and cumin seeds into a small frying pan and dry-fry over a medium heat until the seeds become fragrant and begin to pop. Remove from the heat and use a pestle and mortar to roughly grind them. Set aside.

2. Heat the oil in a large frying pan over a medium heat. Add the onion and leek and sauté until soft, about 5 minutes. Add the garlic, ground spices and a good pinch of salt, stir to mix through, then add the peas and kale or Swiss chard.

3. Pour in the vegetable stock and simmer gently until the vegetables soften, the stock reduces and the mixture thickens, about 5 minutes. Add the spinach and allow to wilt, stirring to mix.

4. Create 4 pockets for the eggs using the back of a spoon, then gently crack an egg into each one. Continue to simmer over a low–medium heat until the egg whites are cooked but the yolks are still wobbly. Remove from the heat and sprinkle over the feta and olives and some freshly ground black pepper. Garnish with lemon wedges, fresh herbs and chilli flakes (if using) and serve with toasted bread.

Note
· To make this gluten free, serve
  with gluten-free bread.

Overnight French toast tray

SERVES | HANDS-ON | HANDS-OFF | SUITABLE FOR
4-6 | 🕐 **15** MINS | 🕐 **30** MINS+ | **V**

Thank your past self the morning after the night before with this sweet and special brunch dish. Prepare it in advance, allowing the bread to soak up all of the sweet milk and then bake, serve piled high with seasonal fruits and lashings of maple syrup. Of course, this can be made and baked in one go, but there's something so relaxing about opening the fridge in the morning and having this ready to go with minimal work needed. Baked in one tray, there's minimal washing up too. Place in the middle of the table and watch it disappear.

60g butter, plus extra for greasing
100g soft light brown sugar
4 tbsp maple syrup
225ml milk
4 large eggs
1 tbsp vanilla bean paste (or use vanilla extract)
1 tsp ground cinnamon
8 slices of bread, halved diagonally
40g demerara sugar

TO SERVE
Strawberries or other berries
Maple syrup
Mint leaves
Icing sugar

Notes
· Use any thick sliced bread. I prefer white sourdough or brioche, or use gluten-free bread.
· Use any milk alternatives.
· Try scattering over chopped nuts before baking. Or dot with 170g cream cheese.

1. Grease a 23 x 33cm baking tin with butter.

2. Melt the butter in a small saucepan over a low heat. Add the light brown sugar and maple syrup and gently stir until the sugar has dissolved. Pour this into the prepared baking tin.

3. Whisk the milk, eggs, vanilla and cinnamon together in a shallow bowl. Fully submerge each triangle of bread into this milky mixture, then arrange in the baking tin, allowing the slices to slightly overlap if necessary. Pour any of the remaining milky mixture over the top. Wrap the tin in foil and refrigerate overnight (or let it soak at room temperature for at least 30 minutes).

4. When you are ready to bake, preheat the oven to 210°C/190°C fan and remove the French toast tray from the fridge. Before it goes in the oven, peel back the foil and sprinkle the top with the demerara sugar. Re-cover with the foil and bake for 20 minutes, then uncover and bake for another 10–15 minutes until the bread is toasted and golden and there's no more liquid in the tin.

5. Remove from the oven and leave to slightly cool before serving. Serve warm, topped with berries, maple syrup, mint leaves and a dusting of icing sugar.

LIGHT, FRESH & FLOURISH

LIGHT, FRESH & FLOURISH

This chapter is all about capturing the beauty of simplicity. Too often with life and with food, we overcomplicate things and think that 'more is better'. More ingredients, more techniques, more steps. A good, well-balanced recipe to me comes down to well-paired flavours, textures and colours.

This needn't be complicated and actually stripping the ingredients list of unnecessary extras and keeping methods straightforward and simple – regardless of how advanced the techniques or recipes are – is the real skill. What makes the biggest difference are the small touches. The finishing herbs, that extra splash of balsamic vinegar, the dressing or dipping sauce. Things we often overlook in an effort to achieve a greater bigger picture.

When I think of light and fresh, I don't think of bland salads, low-fat dressings or children's portion sizes. I think of an abundance of radiant, fresh ingredients and colourful vegetables, vibrant and bright herbs that all help to bring a dish to life. I want to finish eating these meals feeling satiated and energised, not unsatiated, like I've missed out or settled for second best.

Light, fresh and flourishing recipes aren't only synonymous with the warmer, summer months. They can be

'Don't postpone joy until you have learned all of your lessons. Joy IS the lesson.'

enjoyed throughout the year, swapping in vegetables and herbs that are in season for autumn variations. Then warmed lentils and roasted root vegetables are a great base for winter months and can be made in bulk at the start of the week, to help keep the kitchen – and daily life – uncomplicated, but without compromising on the flavours or our experience.

I also wanted these recipes to be easily transportable. These are all perfect for work lunches, picnics or even bring-a-dish parties.

Spinach, pea and potato soup with Parmesan crisps

Roasted tomato, butter bean and basil soup

Roasted potato and green lentil salad with honey, lemon and mustard dressing

Nectarine and burrata salad with quick garlic croutons and a balsamic dressing

Orchard salad with apples, cranberries and candied pecans

Caesar salad with a light and zingy yoghurt dressing

Warm lentil salad with roasted pumpkin, fresh herbs and a lemon maple dressing

Mango, avocado and lime rice-paper rolls with a tahini dip

Bacon and 3-cheese quiche with a hash-brown crust

Nectarine and burrata salad with quick garlic croutons and a balsamic dressing

SERVES | TIME TO MAKE | SUITABLE FOR
4 | 🕐 20 MINS | Ⓥ

The sweetness of stone fruits is enhanced when grilled, giving a beautiful caramelised, smoky flavour. Alongside creamy burrata and a simple, sticky balsamic dressing, this salad only has a handful of ingredients and is quick to pull together, proving that there really can be so much beauty (and flavour) in simplicity. Top with easy garlic croutons for lots of contrasting textures too.

2 slices of white bread
2 garlic cloves, halved
250g bag of rocket
Handful of basil leaves
3 just-ripe nectarines, stoned and cut into wedges
2 tbsp olive oil
1 ball of burrata (or use 200g mozzarella pearls)
Pinch of chilli flakes (optional)

FOR THE DRESSING
3 tbsp extra-virgin olive oil
2 tbsp honey
1 tbsp balsamic vinegar
Juice of ½ lemon
Salt and freshly ground black pepper

Notes
· Salads with fresh fruit are best eaten on the day but will keep for a few hours in the fridge if you want to make ahead.
· Use other stone fruits such as plums, peaches and apricots for seasonal twists.
· To make this gluten free, use gluten-free bread for the croutons.

1. Start by making the croutons. Grill (or toast) the slices of bread until golden. Once toasted and while still hot, rub the halved garlic cloves over each side, then use a sharp knife to slice the bread into cubes.

2. Make the dressing by combining all the ingredients in a small bowl or mug and whisk together with a fork.

3. Toss the rocket and three-quarters of the basil together in a serving dish and set aside until you're ready to assemble the salad.

4. Place a griddle pan or large non-stick frying pan over a high heat. Put the nectarine wedges into a bowl, drizzle over the olive oil and use your hands to lightly coat the fruit in the oil. Once the pan is hot, place the nectarines cut side down in the pan. Cook for 2 minutes on each side until golden and charred.

5. To assemble the salad, lay the griddled fruit over the rocket and basil, then use your hands to tear over the burrata. Scatter over the croutons and then drizzle over dressing. Finish with a grind of black pepper, a generous pinch of salt, the chilli flakes (if using) and the remaining basil leaves.

Mango, avocado and lime rice-paper rolls with a tahini dip

SERVES | TIME TO MAKE | SUITABLE FOR
6 | 🕐 20 MINS | VE

I love the variety of possibilities that come with using rice-paper rolls – their sheer appearance means you can see all of the fresh, vibrant vegetables and herbs shining through. Chilli, mango and lime is one of my favourite uplifting flavour combinations and the tahini dipping sauce is incredible too.

12 sheets of Vietnamese rice paper
Bunch of fresh mint, leaves picked
Bunch of fresh coriander, leaves picked
½ purple cabbage, finely shredded
2 avocados, peeled, stoned and sliced
2 mangoes, diced
Lime wedges

FOR THE DRESSING
120g tahini
1 tbsp soy sauce
2 garlic cloves, finely chopped
4 tbsp maple syrup
Pinch of chilli flakes

1. Prepare all your fillings first and lay everything out in front of you like a production line – once the rice-paper rolls are wet, you need to work quickly so it helps to have everything set up beforehand.

2. Fill a shallow bowl with water and dip one sheet of rice paper in for a few seconds. It will still feel quite firm when you first take it out of the water but it will continue to soften up while you work to fill it.

3. Use a teaspoon to heap some of each filling in, making a line down the centre. Start with the herbs and red cabbage to make a soft bed for the other ingredients to lie on. Top with the sliced avocado and mango, a squeeze of lime and then roll up like burritos, tucking the short sides in first and then rolling up to enclose the filling.

4. Once you've made all of your wraps, set them aside to let the flavours mingle while you make the tahini dipping sauce. Combine the tahini with the soy sauce, garlic and maple syrup in a bowl, adding a few dashes of water to loosen, if needed. Finish with a pinch of chilli flakes.

5. Serve the wraps with the dipping sauce and extra wedges of lime.

Notes
· These are best enjoyed fresh and on the day they're made.
· Use leftover vegetables such as carrot or cucumber or other fillings such as shredded chicken (see page 88) or toasted chickpeas.
· To make this gluten-free, use tamari instead of soy sauce.

Spinach, pea and potato soup with Parmesan crisps

SERVES	TIME TO MAKE	SUITABLE FOR
4	🕐 40 MINS	

Simple, soothing and delicious. High in both fibre and iron, this is a satisfying and satiating soup that won't leave you feeling weighed down. Potatoes give this soup its thick, creamy texture. I love Parmesan crisps and they're really simple to make. They look like impressive, intricate lace patterns and add a nice, salty crunch contrast to the smooth soup.

3 tbsp olive oil
1 yellow onion, diced
1 leek, diced
2 garlic cloves, finely chopped
2 celery sticks, diced
2 white potatoes, peeled and diced
1 litre vegetable stock
250g baby spinach
120g frozen peas
Squeeze of lemon juice
Salt and freshly ground black pepper
Chopped parsley or chives, to garnish

FOR THE PARMESAN CRISPS
80g Parmesan cheese, grated
Freshly ground black pepper

Notes
· To store, cool and refrigerate in an airtight container for up to 5 days or freeze for up to 3 months.
· Store the baked Parmesan crisps at room temperature in an airtight container for up to 1 week, until you're ready to enjoy.

1. Heat the oil in a heavy-based saucepan over a medium heat. Sauté the onion and leek for 3–5 minutes until soft and translucent. Add the garlic, celery and potatoes. Reduce the heat to low and allow the vegetables to sweat, lid on, for about 10 minutes, stirring often.

2. Pour in the stock and increase the heat to bring it to a gentle simmer. Cook for 15 minutes until the potatoes are soft and tender when pricked with a fork.

3. Reduce the heat to low and add the spinach and peas. Cook for 3 minutes until the spinach has wilted, then use a hand-held stick blender to blitz the soup until smooth. Taste and season with salt and pepper.

4. Meanwhile, for the Parmesan crisps, preheat the oven to 220°C/200°C fan and line a baking sheet with baking paper. Use heaped tablespoons of Parmesan to create 8 mounds on the baking tray. Roughly shape into circles (or use a circular cookie cutter as a guide for a cleaner shape), press down gently on each mound with the back of the spoon and finish each one with some cracks of black pepper.

6. Bake for 5–8 minutes until crisp and golden. Remove and cool completely before peeling off the paper.

7. Just before serving the soup, add a squeeze of lemon juice and sprinkle with the fresh herbs. Serve with the Parmesan crisps.

Roasted tomato, butter bean and basil soup

SERVES | TIME TO MAKE | SUITABLE FOR
4 | 🕐 40 MINS | ❄ VE GF

6 large tomatoes, quartered
4 garlic cloves, left whole
5 tbsp olive oil
1 tbsp balsamic vinegar
1 tsp dried thyme
1 yellow onion, diced
4 tbsp tomato purée
1 tsp dried oregano
1 litre vegetable stock
400g tin butter beans, drained
   and rinsed
Handful of fresh basil leaves, plus
   a few extra to garnish
Salt and freshly ground black
   pepper

Notes
*· Taste the soup for seasoning as
  you go. I always find tomato-based
  dishes need a little more salt.*
*· To store, cool and refrigerate in an
  airtight container for up to 5 days or
  freeze for up to 3 months.*
*· For soup on the go, picnics or
  packed lunches, use a good-quality
  Thermos flask. Pour the soup in while
  it's still hot and it will stay warm all
  day until you're ready to enjoy.*

Roasting the tomatoes brings out their sweetness and intensifies the flavour. Butter beans add a creamy texture and are packed with fibre to keep us feeling fuller for longer. Forget the tinned, watery cans of tomato soup that leave your stomach rumbling after an hour (or require at least half a loaf of bread accompanying the soup to fill you up). Enjoy this as it is, or with Parmesan crisps (see page 42) or (a childhood favourite) with a slice of grilled cheese on toast.

1. Preheat the oven to 220°C/200°C fan.

2. Spread the quartered tomatoes and whole garlic cloves out in a roasting tin and drizzle over 4 tablespoons of the olive oil and the balsamic vinegar. Scatter over the thyme and some salt and pepper. Roast for 25–30 minutes until the tomatoes and softened and the juices are bubbling.

3. Meanwhile, heat the remaining tablespoon olive oil in a heavy-based saucepan over a medium heat. Add the onion and sauté for 3–5 minutes until soft and translucent. Add the tomato purée and sprinkle in the dried oregano, using your fingers to rub and warm the herb (this will help to release its flavour). Cook for 2–3 minutes, stirring to mix everything together.

4. Pour in the stock and beans and bring everything to a gentle simmer. Use a large spoon to transfer the roasted tomatoes and garlic to the pot. Pour in the remaining tomato juices and olive oil from the roasting tin as these will be bursting with flavour. Remove from the heat and taste for seasoning. Add in a handful of fresh, torn basil leaves and use a hand-held stick blender to pulse the soup until you're happy with the consistency – I like mine quite chunky.

5. Serve with a few extra basil leaves scattered over the top and a grind of black pepper.

Warm lentil salad with roasted pumpkin, fresh herbs and a lemon maple dressing

SERVES | TIME TO MAKE | SUITABLE FOR
4 | 40 MINS | VE GF

Roasting the pumpkin in cinnamon gives a sweet lift to this earthy and nourishing dish, which can be enjoyed warm in cooler climates, or served cold in warmer months. Lentils make this dish more satiating, and packed with fibre, they also act as a sponge to soak up and carry the flavours of the incredible dressing. Finished with crunchy nuts, seeds and lots of fresh herbs, this is a simple dish but a real crowd-pleaser with so many flavours and textures to notice in each bite.

1kg pumpkin, sliced into 1cm wedges (skin on)
2 tbsp olive oil
2 tsp ground cinnamon
1 tsp salt
120g rocket
120g spinach
1 red onion, thinly sliced
Handful of mixed herbs (I like parsley, mint and basil leaves)
400g tin lentils, drained and rinsed
40g walnuts, roughly chopped
30g pumpkin seeds

FOR THE DRESSING
3 tbsp extra-virgin olive oil
2 tbsp maple syrup
1 tbsp balsamic vinegar
2 garlic cloves, finely chopped
Juice of ½ lemon
3 tsp thyme leaves
Salt and freshly ground black pepper

Notes
· Store in the fridge in an airtight container for up to 3 days.
· Swap the pumpkin for butternut squash or sweet potato.

1. Preheat the oven to 200°C/180°C fan. Arrange the pumpkin wedges in a single layer in a baking tray (you may need 2 trays) and drizzle over the olive oil. Sprinkle over the cinnamon and salt and roast for 30 minutes, using tongs or a fork to turn the wedges over halfway through.

2. In a small bowl or mug, whisk the dressing ingredients together with a fork and set aside.

3. Toss the salad leaves together with the red onion and most of the herbs in a large bowl.

4. Warm the lentils in a saucepan with a dash of water so they don't stick together, then season with salt and pepper and mix through the salad leaves with half of the dressing.

5. To assemble the salad, tip the salad leaves and lentils into a serving bowl and top with the roasted wedges of pumpkin. Scatter over the chopped walnuts and pumpkin seeds and the remaining herbs. Finally, drizzle over the remaining dressing.

Roasted potato and green lentil salad with honey, lemon and mustard dressing

SERVES | TIME TO MAKE | SUITABLE FOR
4 | ⏲ **45 MINS** |

The vibrant, zingy dressing in this recipe really is the small touch that makes the dish. Poured over still piping hot roasted potatoes, which act like a sponge to soak up all the flavours. Super-simple to make with only a handful of ingredients and packed with flavour, this tastes even better the next day too. Say no to shit salads!

900g new potatoes (or Jersey Royals if you can get them)
2 tbsp extra-virgin olive oil
1 tsp salt
390g tin cooked lentils (I use green), drained and rinsed
250g spinach
Handful of parsley, leaves finely chopped
Handful of dill, leaves finely chopped

FOR THE DRESSING
3 tbsp extra-virgin olive oil
2 tbsp honey
1 tsp wholegrain mustard
Juice of 1 lemon
Salt and freshly ground black pepper

1. Preheat the oven to 220°C/200°C fan.

2. Cut any larger potatoes in half so they're all similar in size and place them in a roasting tin with the olive oil and salt. Use your hands to toss the potatoes so that they're evenly covered. Roast in the oven for 40 minutes, giving the tin a shake halfway through.

3. While the potatoes are roasting, make the dressing: combine all the ingredients in a small jar and give it a good shake to mix. Taste and season with salt and pepper.

4. Once the potatoes are ready (they should still be firm but a metal fork will easily pierce their skins and flesh), remove from the oven and tip the lentils and spinach into the roasting tin (the spinach leaves will start to steam and wilt in the heat – which is what we want).

5. Finally, pour over the dressing and mix well, coating all of the potatoes. Scatter over the fresh parsley and dill before serving.

Notes
· *Enjoy warm or cold – the potatoes and lentils soak up the dressing so it's great the following day too.*
· *Serves 4 as a meal or 6 as a side. Crumble over some feta or serve with griddled marinated chicken (see page 66) or pan-fried salmon fillet.*
· *To make this vegan, swap the honey in the dressing for maple syrup.*

Orchard salad with apples, cranberries and candied pecans

SERVES | TIME TO MAKE | SUITABLE FOR
4 | ⏲ **20** MINS |

Inspired by one of my favourite spots in the Cotswolds, Daylesford Farm, whose kale salad I adore. A nutritional superstar, this dark, leafy green is packed with nutrients including more than 100 per cent of the recommended daily requirement of Vitamins A, K, C per serving. Wildly misunderstood, after a little love and a quick massage – in this case with olive oil and lemon to help to break down its tough and bitter exterior – kale is coupled here with sweet and crunchy apples, cranberries and candied pecans and a sticky, tangy and sweet dressing. If you've had a bad experience with kale, I implore you to give this a go.

125g kale
Juice of 1 lemon
2 tbsp olive oil
125g baby spinach
2 apples
80g dried cranberries

FOR THE CANDIED PECANS
80g pecans
1 tbsp butter
4 tbsp soft light brown sugar
Pinch of sea salt

FOR THE DRESSING
2 tbsp olive oil
2 tbsp honey
1 tbsp apple cider vinegar
1 tbsp wholegrain mustard

Notes
· *Store for up to 3 days in the fridge. Great to make ahead, kale holds its shape and texture, avoiding the salad-bag slime of sensitive leaves.*
· *Candied nuts can be stored in an airtight container for up to 2 weeks.*
· *Try pear instead of apple, or swap pecans for candied walnuts or flaked almonds.*

1. In a small bowl or mug, whisk the dressing ingredients together with a fork and set aside.

2. Lay a sheet of baking paper on a heatproof surface to pour the hot sugared nuts on to – make sure it's close by.

3. Toast the pecans in a dry frying pan over a high heat for 2–3 minutes until they smell nutty but before they brown. Remove from the heat and add the butter and sugar, stirring until dissolved. Pour the mixture on to the baking paper, sprinkle with salt and leave to cool.

4. Put the kale into a large bowl, pour the lemon juice and oil over and with clean hands toss and rub (or 'massage') this into the leaves. After 2–3 minutes the leaves will start to soften while holding their shape. Throw in the baby spinach and toss to mix through. Chop the apples into matchsticks and toss into the leaves with the cranberries; lemon prevents browning.

5. When you're ready to serve, pour the dressing over the salad and crumble over the cool candied nuts.

Caesar salad with a light and zingy yoghurt dressing

SERVES 4 | **TIME TO MAKE** 🕐 **35 MINS**

A true classic, Caesar salad was my first real 'salad' experience, though usually from the food-to-go supermarket aisle, light on the crunchy bacon and croutons (the best bits) and weighed down by a heavy PVA-glue-like dressing. I've created this zingy, lighter lemon dressing with natural yoghurt, so you still get a creamy dressing to pull everything together without coating the salad leaves in a thick, heavy paste. The croutons are finished off in the oven here, doused in olive oil – they're one of the main stars here, not just a finishing touch.

3 slices of white bread
3 garlic cloves, halved
2 tbsp olive oil
140g smoked streaky bacon
1 large head of romaine lettuce, thinly sliced
4 tbsp shaved Parmesan cheese
1 tbsp snipped chives, to garnish

FOR THE DRESSING
250g natural yoghurt
Juice of 1 lemon
2 tbsp olive oil
1 tbsp honey
1 tsp Dijon mustard
1 garlic clove, finely chopped
60g Parmesan cheese, finely grated
2 anchovies, from a tin
Salt and freshly ground black pepper

Notes
· Store salad and dressing separately in airtight containers in the fridge for up to 3 days.
· Serve as a side or main – try with hard-boiled eggs, grilled salmon or marinated chicken (see page 66).

1. Start by making the croutons. Preheat the oven to 200°/180°C fan and then toast the bread until lightly golden. Once toasted and while still hot, rub the halved garlic cloves over each side. Use a sharp knife to slice into cubes, scatter into a baking tray and drizzle over the olive oil, using your hands to toss the cubed toast in the oil. Sprinkle generously with salt and then bake for 6–8 minutes until deep golden brown and crisp.

2. Make the dressing by combining all the ingredients in a small food processor and blitzing until smooth. Add more yoghurt, or a splash of milk, to loosen.

3. Preheat the grill to high and then grill the bacon until golden and crispy. Remove from the heat and use scissors to roughly snip into smaller pieces.

4. To assemble the salad, toss the sliced lettuce leaves with a few tablespoons of the dressing. Top with the bacon and croutons and spoon over some more dressing. Finish with a generous sprinkling of Parmesan cheese, the snipped chives and a few grinds of black pepper. Serve with the remaining dressing on the side.

Bacon and 3-cheese quiche with a hash-brown crust

SERVES | TIME TO MAKE | SUITABLE FOR
6–8 | ⏱ 1 HR | ❄ GF

Swapping the usual savoury pastry case for a thin, golden and crispy hash brown crust was a revelation. I first experienced this phenomenon on a menu in Edinburgh, one of my favourite cities. Here I've paired it with a classic quiche Lorraine filling of onion, eggs, bacon and cheese. Perfect for picnics or for feeding a crowd as you can make this ahead of time.

FOR THE CRUST
600g white potatoes (King Edwards or Russet), peeled
2 tbsp butter, plus extra for greasing
60g Parmesan cheese, grated
Salt and freshly ground black pepper

FOR THE FILLING
1 tbsp butter
1 yellow onion, diced
8 rashers of smoked streaky bacon
2 garlic cloves, finely chopped
80g Cheddar cheese, grated
60g Gruyère cheese, grated
6 large eggs
150ml double cream
¼ tsp freshly grated nutmeg
1 tbsp snipped chives

1. Preheat the oven to 220°C/200°C fan.

2. For the hash-brown crust, grate the potatoes and tip into a colander, then rinse under the cold tap for about 30 seconds. Lay some kitchen paper on the worktop and shake the colander to get rid of dripping water. Use your hands to squeeze excess water out of small handfuls of potato, then spread it on the kitchen paper. Repeat until all the potato has been rinsed and squeezed. You want to get rid of as much water as possible.

3. Melt the butter in a large saucepan over a low heat. Remove from the heat and tip in the potato and Parmesan and season. Mix to combine.

4. Lightly grease a 23cm round baking dish (or ovenproof frying pan) with butter (or use cooking spray). Press the hash-brown mixture into the bottom and up the sides of the pan, ensuring there are no gaps. Use a tumbler with a flat base to press down, compressing the crust and creating an even layer. Bake in the oven for about 30 minutes until lightly golden brown.

5. Meanwhile, prepare the filling. Melt the butter over a medium heat and sauté the onion until soft and translucent, about 5 minutes. Use scissors to snip the bacon into the pan, then add the garlic and sauté until the bacon is golden (but not crispy). Tip the cooked bacon, onion and garlic into the baked hash-brown crust and sprinkle over two-thirds of the cheese.

6. Whisk the eggs, cream and nutmeg together in a large jug and season with salt and pepper. Pour this into the hash-brown crust, covering the bacon, onion and cheese. Sprinkle over the remaining cheese and return to the oven. Reduce the temperature to 200°C/180°C fan and bake for 30 minutes until the filling is just set.

7. Remove from the oven and allow to cool slightly before scattering over chopped chives and some freshly ground black pepper. Cut into slices and serve.

QUICK & SIMPLE

QUICK & SIMPLE

This chapter celebrates dishes that can come together in no time. Being adaptable and flexible with life is one of the most valuable characteristics I've come to embrace: 'The only constant in life, is change.'

Whether that means a last-minute meeting you have to prepare for, an unanticipated catch-up with a friend or the opportunity to invite people over for dinner at short notice, these recipes can be whipped up with no prior preparation needed.

You'll find stir-fries, quick Thai curries and fish dishes in this chapter – all quick to cook and bursting with flavour (short on time doesn't have to mean short on flavour). Choose a handful of your favourite recipes from this chapter and make sure you keep those ingredients that crop up time and again in your capsule food cupboard (see page 13) and extra cuts of meat, fish or chicken in your freezer.

'Find what it is that you love. Then do more of that.'

I'm all for sensible short cuts and these recipes all work brilliantly with pouched rice or lentils (see page 13); I stock up on a variety of flavours so that when I'm short on time I still have plenty of options. Many of these recipes are freezer-friendly too, which means that I can stash any leftovers away for days and weeks when I know time is not on my side. Just defrost the night before and reheat the following day.

Lentil-loaded nachos
Panko and Parmesan-crusted salmon
Crunchy vegetable stir-fry with maple tamari sauce
Chinese-style beef and ginger stir-fry
Green Thai chicken curry
Red Thai chickpea curry
Marinated chicken 4 ways
Salmon and ginger fishcakes
Halloumi, chilli and mint lentil salad with a lemon tahini dressing

Lentil-loaded nachos

SERVES | TIME TO MAKE | SUITABLE FOR
4 | 20 MINS |

Lentils act as a sponge to soak up all the flavours here and add lots of texture and fibre to contrast with the crispy nachos. Make sure you include the enlivening spices here in your capsule food cupboard (see page 13) and throw together in fewer than 20 minutes when you have friends coming over. Tortilla chips and pouched lentils, with their long shelf life, are great storecupboard essentials that can be useful in so many dishes.

1 tbsp olive oil
1 small onion, finely diced
2 garlic cloves, finely chopped
2 tsp ground cumin
1 tsp paprika
250g pouch of cooked lentils
200g salted tortilla chips
80g Cheddar cheese, grated
2 spring onions, sliced on the
    diagonal
1 jalapeño pepper, sliced
Handful of parsley or coriander
Salt

TO SERVE
Guacamole
Sour cream
Salsa
Lime wedges

1. Preheat the grill to high.

2. Warm the oil in a large saucepan over a high heat. Add the onion and sauté for a few minutes until it begins to soften, then stir in the garlic. Turn the heat down to medium and add the spices and a good pinch of salt. Add the lentils and use a wooden spoon to break them up and mix with the spices, onion and garlic. Remove from the heat.

3. In an ovenproof dish, layer handfuls of the tortilla chips with the lentil mixture and grated cheese. Place under the grill for 3–5 minutes until the cheese starts to melt and bubble.

4. Remove from the grill and sprinkle over the spring onions, jalapeño and herbs. Serve with dips and lime wedges on the side.

Notes
· Use any other favourite vegetables to add colour and flavour to the sautéed onion – peppers, sweetcorn (tinned, fresh or frozen) both work well and add crunch. Mushrooms or diced tomatoes can bulk out the lentils and add a deeper, earthier flavour.
· To make this gluten free, use gluten-free tortilla chips.

Panko and Parmesan-crusted salmon

SERVES **TIME TO MAKE**
4 **20 MINS**

Panko, Parmesan, thyme and lemon pack loads of flavour and texture into this crusted salmon dish. The crust is pushed into the top of salmon fillets, then the skin is pan-fried until golden and crispy and then finished off in the oven. Crunchy on the outside and buttery soft in the middle.

4 salmon fillets (skin on)
2 tsp Dijon mustard
4 tsp honey
60g panko breadcrumbs
60g Parmesan cheese, coarsely grated (not the fine dust)
2 tbsp finely chopped parsley (leaves and stalks)
2 tsp thyme leaves
Zest of ½ lemon
4 tbsp olive oil
Salt and freshly ground black pepper
Lemon wedges, to serve

1. Preheat the oven to 220°C/200°C fan. Remove the salmon from the fridge and pat dry with kitchen paper to remove any excess moisture. This will give a crispy skin and allow the breadcrumbs to stick more easily to the top of the fillet.

2. Mix together the Dijon mustard and honey in a small bowl. This will be the 'glue' for our breadcrumb mix.

3. In another small bowl, mix together the breadcrumbs, Parmesan, parsley, thyme, lemon zest and season with salt and pepper. Pour over 2 tablespoons of the olive oil and stir to combine.

4. Smear the honey mustard mixture on to the top of each salmon fillet, then use your hands to press the breadcrumb mixture on top, pressing down firmly.

5. Heat the remaining 2 tablespoons of olive oil in an ovenproof frying pan or saucepan over a medium–high heat. Once hot, add the salmon fillets, skin-side down, and let them cook for 4 minutes until the topping is crisp.

6. Transfer the pan to the oven and bake for 6–8 minutes until the panko crust is golden. Cover with foil and allow to rest for 10 minutes. Serve with lemon wedges.

Note
· Store leftover salmon fillets in an airtight container in the fridge for up to 3 days – they are great flaked over a simple salad the next day.

Crunchy vegetable stir-fry with maple tamari sauce

SERVES | TIME TO MAKE | SUITABLE FOR
4 | 25 MINS | VE GF

600g mixed mushrooms (oyster, cremini, button, shiitake and/or enoki), roughly chopped or quartered into bite-sized pieces
2 tbsp peanut oil (or vegetable oil)
80g sugar snap peas
1 yellow pepper, sliced
120g broccolini, thick stems sliced lengthways
1 red chilli, deseeded and diced (optional)
2 pak choi, sliced

FOR THE SAUCE
2 garlic cloves, crushed
3cm piece of fresh ginger, peeled and finely chopped
4 tbsp maple syrup
4 tbsp tamari
2 tbsp sesame oil
2 tbsp water
Juice of 1 lime

TO SERVE
Rice or rice noodles
Coriander leaves
Chopped toasted cashews (see Notes)

Stir-frying vegetables keeps them vibrant in colour, flavour and texture. They should still have a bite to them but a lot of it comes down to the timing. Rather than throwing everything into the pan in one go, this vegetable stir-fry cooks the mushrooms separately so that they're golden and their texture is meaty, rather than allowing everything to meld into one soggy bowl – one of the most common mistakes with a stir-fry!

1. Put all the sauce ingredients into a large bowl and stir to combine, then taste and adjust with more maple syrup, tamari or lime juice as you like. Add the mushrooms to the marinade and set aside for 15 minutes while you prepare the other vegetables.

2. Heat the oil in a wok or large saucepan over a high heat. Add the sugar snap peas, yellow pepper, broccolini and chilli (if using). Stir fry for 3–4 minutes until the vegetables are tender but still hold some bite. Tip them on to a plate and set aside.

3. Return the pan to the heat and add the mushrooms and sauce. Stir-fry over a high heat until golden brown, about 4 minutes. Add the pak choi for the last minute, allowing it to wilt slightly, then return the vegetables to the pan and toss everything together to coat with the sauce.

4. Remove from the heat and serve immediately over rice or noodles, scattered with coriander leaves and chopped cashews.

Notes
· To toast cashews, tip them into a dry frying pan and place over a medium heat for a few minutes until they turn golden brown. Shake the pan occasionally so they toast evenly and keep an eye on them as they burn quickly!
· Store leftovers in an airtight container in the fridge for up to 3 days.

Chinese-style beef and ginger stir-fry

SERVES TIME TO MAKE SUITABLE FOR
4 | 25 MINS | DF

If I'm pressed for time, fresh, light and fragrant stir-fries are my usual go-to. I used to reach for the supermarket ready-prepared packs but I much prefer making my own now. Freshly sliced vegetables pack way more flavour and crunch than pre-chopped and it means you can choose your favourite combinations. This delicious, Chinese-inspired sauce comes together in no time and beats any supermarket sauce pouch. Leave the beef to marinate in the sauce and let the marinade do all the hard work while you prepare the vegetables.

500g beef rump (or skirt fillet), sliced into strips
4 tbsp peanut oil (or vegetable oil)
4 spring onions, diced
2 garlic cloves, crushed
1 red chilli, deseeded and diced (optional)
6 baby corn, sliced in half lengthways
80g sugar snap peas
1 red pepper, sliced
1 green pepper, sliced

FOR THE STIR-FRY SAUCE
5cm piece of fresh ginger, peeled and finely chopped
4 tbsp soy sauce
2 tbsp oyster sauce
2 tbsp rice vinegar
1 tbsp soft light brown sugar
1 tbsp sesame oil
4 tbsp cornflour, mixed with 2 tbsp water to make a paste

TO SERVE
Rice or noodles
Coriander leaves
Sesame seeds

1. Mix all the sauce ingredients, except for the cornflour paste, together in a small bowl. Add 2 tablespoons of this sauce to a ziplock bag and add the beef strips, turning to coat in the marinade. Set aside for 10–15 minutes while you prepare the vegetables. Meanwhile, add 200ml warm water to the remaining sauce in the bowl (we'll use this at the end).

2. Heat the oil in a wok or large saucepan over a high heat. Add the spring onions, garlic and chilli (if using) and sauté for 1 minute, then add the marinated beef and cook until browned all over.

3. Add the baby corn, sugar snap peas and peppers and stir-fry for another minute before adding the stir-fry sauce and cornflour paste. Cook for 1–2 minutes until the sauce has thickened and the beef is cooked through.

4. Serve immediately with rice or noodles, garnished with coriander leaves and a sprinkle of sesame seeds.

Notes
· Store in an airtight container in the fridge for up to 3 days.
· To make this gluten free, use tamari instead of soy sauce and serve with gluten-free noodles or rice.

Green Thai chicken curry

SERVES | TIME TO MAKE | SUITABLE FOR
4 | ⏱ 25 MINS | ❄ GF DF

This is my favourite Thai curry, with its incredibly fragrant sauce flavoured with ginger, lemongrass and kaffir lime leaves for a light and refreshing flavour. It won't leave you feeling stodgy like so many takeaway alternatives and, even better, it comes together quicker than ordering one online.

6 tbsp green Thai curry paste
2 garlic cloves, finely chopped
5cm piece of fresh ginger, peeled and grated
1 tbsp lemongrass paste
2 tbsp coconut oil
250ml chicken or vegetable stock
400ml tin coconut milk
2 tsp Thai fish sauce
1 tbsp soft light brown sugar
3 kaffir lime leaves, torn in half
1 lemongrass stalk, white end bashed
350g chicken thigh fillets
120g mangetout
Pinch of salt
Juice of 1 lime

TO SERVE
Coriander leaves
Thai basil leaves
Chopped toasted peanuts (see Notes)

1. Put the green Thai curry paste, garlic, ginger and lemongrass paste into a bowl and stir together until combined. Set aside.

2. Heat the coconut oil in a heavy-based saucepan over a medium–high heat, then add the curry paste and cook for 2 minutes, stirring to release the fragrance. Pour in the stock and coconut milk and bring to a gentle simmer.

3. Stir in the fish sauce, brown sugar, kaffir lime leaves and lemongrass and cook for another few minutes. Add the chicken thighs and cook over a medium heat for 12 minutes until the chicken is cooked.

4. Add the mangetout and simmer for another 3 minutes, then season with a pinch of salt. Squeeze in the lime juice.

5. Serve with jasmine rice with coriander and Thai basil leaves torn over the top. Finish with a sprinkle of chopped peanuts.

Notes
· This delicious curry isn't meant to have a thick, heavy sauce. It's best served with steamed jasmine rice, to soak up the delicious extra sauce.
· To toast peanuts, tip them into a dry frying pan and place over a medium heat for a few minutes until they turn golden brown. Shake the pan occasionally so they toast evenly and keep an eye on them as they burn quickly!
· Store leftovers in an airtight container in the fridge for up to 3 days.
· Freeze for up to 3 months; defrost overnight in the fridge and then reheat until piping hot.

Red Thai chickpea curry

SERVES | TIME TO MAKE | SUITABLE FOR
4 | 25 MINS |

Typically hotter than green or yellow Thai curry, this is packed with vegetables and chickpeas, which carry the flavours so well.

6 tbsp red Thai curry paste
2 garlic cloves, finely chopped
5cm piece of fresh ginger, peeled and grated
1 tbsp lemongrass paste
2 tbsp coconut oil
1 yellow onion
250ml vegetable stock
400ml tin coconut milk
700g butternut squash, peeled and cubed
3 kaffir lime leaves, torn in half
400g tin chickpeas, drained and rinsed
2 tbsp tamari
2 tbsp maple syrup
4 large handfuls of spinach
Juice of 1 lime
Salt

TO SERVE
Jasmine rice
Coriander and basil
Chopped cashews

1. Mix the red Thai curry paste with the garlic, ginger and lemongrass paste in a small bowl. Set aside.

2. Heat the coconut oil in a heavy-based saucepan over a medium–high heat. Add the onion and sauté until soft and translucent, 3–5 minutes

3. Add the curry paste and cook for another 2 minutes, until it releases its aroma. Add the stock and coconut milk and bring to a gentle simmer, then add the butternut squash and torn kaffir lime leaves and stir through.

4. Cook at a gentle simmer for 20 minutes until the squash is tender when pricked with a fork. Add the chickpeas, tamari and maple syrup and simmer for another 5 minutes.

5. Remove from the heat and use a hand-held stick blender to roughly blitz, leaving some whole chunks. Add the spinach and cover the pan with a lid, allowing the spinach to wilt while it cools down slightly.

6. Season with a pinch of salt, then add some torn basil or coriander leaves (if using) and lime juice. Serve with jasmine rice and finish by sprinkling with more herbs and chopped cashews.

Notes
· Store leftovers in an airtight container in the fridge for up to 3 days.
· Freeze for up to 3 months in a suitable container. Defrost overnight in the fridge and then reheat until piping hot.

Marinated chicken 4 ways

SERVES | TIME TO MAKE | SUITABLE FOR
4 | **30 MINS** | **DF**

A really simple way to keep food interesting is to switch up the small things – the sauces, the marinades, the spreads. If you're a creature of habit and routine but are interested in extending your recipe repertoire, this is a great place to start. These marinades come together in a few minutes and do all the work for you. Marinate for as little as 30 minutes to soak up the flavours or prepare a few hours or the night before and you can have juicy, flavoursome chicken ready whenever you are. I use these marinades on chicken breasts, which can often be dry when cooked plain; flattening the chicken breasts before marinating allows them to absorb more of the marinade and also reduces the cooking time.

Notes
- *Marinate for as little as 30 minutes, although I find that a good 3 hours will give you the best flavour; overnight is ideal.*
- *Use these marinades for other main dishes, such as steak or firm tofu.*
- *To make these gluten free, use tamari instead of soy sauce.*

1. Before marinating, flatten each chicken breast by placing between 2 sheets of baking paper and bashing with a rolling pin until an even thickness.

2. Mix up all the marinade ingredients and then add to a ziplock bag or large bowl with the chicken. Cover with cling film and leave for at least 30 minutes.

3. Heat a non-stick frying pan or griddle pan over a medium–high heat. Fry the chicken for 3–4 minutes each side until golden brown on the outside and cooked through. Leave to rest for 5 minutes before serving.

STICKY SOY AND HONEY CHICKEN

4 chicken breasts
2 tbsp honey
1 tbsp olive oil
4 tbsp soy sauce
Juice of 1 lemon
2 tsp Worcestershire sauce
4 garlic cloves, crushed
Pinch of dried herbs (oregano, rosemary, thyme)
Freshly ground black pepper

LEMONGRASS AND GINGER CHICKEN

4 chicken breasts
2 lemongrass stalks, tough outer layer removed, finely chopped (or use 3 tbsp lemongrass paste)
3 garlic cloves, crushed
Juice of 1 lime
1 tbsp soy sauce
2 tbsp soft light brown sugar
1 tbsp fish sauce
1 tbsp olive oil
5cm piece of fresh ginger, peeled and grated

JERK CHICKEN

4 chicken breasts
2 tsp dried thyme
4 tbsp soy sauce
1 tsp ground allspice
3 tbsp soft light brown sugar
3 garlic cloves, crushed
½ tsp ground cinnamon
½ tsp cayenne pepper
4 tbsp olive oil
Juice of 2 limes
1 Scotch bonnet chilli pepper, finely chopped (optional)
Salt and freshly ground black pepper

COCONUT AND LIME CHICKEN

4 chicken breasts
Thumb-sized piece of fresh ginger, peeled and grated
4 garlic cloves, crushed
200ml full-fat coconut milk
Zest and juice of 2 limes
2 tbsp soft light brown sugar
1 tsp salt
1 tbsp Thai curry paste (green or red)
2 tbsp olive oil

Salmon and ginger fishcakes

SERVES | **TIME TO MAKE** | **SUITABLE FOR**
4 | ⏱ **40 MINS** | ❄ DF

A great way to use up leftover potatoes, fishcakes should be crispy on the outside and soft and flavoursome on the inside.

500g floury potatoes such as King Edward or Maris Piper, peeled and cut into chunks
1 tbsp mayonnaise
1 tbsp finely chopped parsley
Thumb-sized piece of fresh ginger, peeled and grated
½ tbsp olive oil
4 spring onions, thinly sliced
2 x 180g tins sustainably caught salmon, drained
2 tbsp plain flour, plus extra for dusting
2 eggs, beaten
60g breadcrumbs (I like panko)
Salt and freshly ground black pepper
Watercress salad and lemon wedges, to serve

1. Preheat the oven to 220°C/200°C fan and line a baking tray with non-stick baking paper.

2. Add the potatoes to a large saucepan of salted water and bring to the boil. Reduce the heat, cover and simmer for 12–15 minutes under tender, then drain well and leave to steam dry. Mash until smooth, then add the mayonnaise, chopped parsley and ginger.

3. In a small frying pan, heat the olive oil over a medium–high heat, add the spring onions and fry for about 2 minutes until soft. Add these to the large bowl of potatoes and mix together with a good pinch of salt, then fold in the salmon until just combined.

4. Use damp hands to divide the mixture into 8 and roughly shape into even-sized fishcakes.

5. Put the flour on a plate, the eggs in one bowl and the breadcrumbs in another. Dust each fishcake in the flour, then dip into the egg and then gently press them into the breadcrumbs. Place the fishcakes on the lined baking tray and repeat until all of them are evenly coated. Bake for 20 minutes until golden brown and crisp.

6. Serve the fishcakes with a big handful of watercress and lemon wedges for squeezing over.

Notes
· Store in an airtight container for up to 3 days in the fridge.
· To freeze, layer coated but uncooked fishcakes between sheets of baking paper in an airtight container. Freeze for up to 3 months. Bake from frozen, adding a few minutes to the cooking time.

Halloumi, chilli and mint lentil salad with a lemon tahini dressing

SERVES | **TIME TO MAKE** | **SUITABLE FOR**
4 | **20 MINS** | **V** **GF**

I love this salad because it's suited to any season. It originally came together as a bit of a leftover clear-out salad, but I loved the flavour combinations so much I made it into its own recipe. Halloumi, chilli and mint create a classic combination of salt, heat and sweetness. Use whatever fresh herbs you have on hand and swap the halloumi for feta, burrata or mozzarella for a twist.

250g halloumi, sliced
1 tbsp olive oil
1 red onion, thinly sliced
2 garlic cloves, finely chopped
250g pouch of cooked lentils
Handful of mixed salad leaves
Handful of fresh mint leaves
1 red chilli, deseeded and diced
30g pecans, roughly chopped

FOR THE DRESSING
3 tbsp tahini
2 tbsp olive oil
1 tbsp maple syrup
Juice of 1 lemon
Salt and freshly ground black pepper

1. Preheat the grill to high and line a baking tray with foil. Add the sliced halloumi and grill for 3–4 minutes on each side until golden.

2. To make the dressing, combine the tahini in a mug with a splash of cold water to loosen. Then add everything else and whisk together with a fork.

3. Warm the olive oil in a saucepan over a medium heat. Add the red onion and sauté until it starts to soften. Add the garlic and a good pinch of salt and stir through, then add the lentils and use a wooden spoon to break them up and mix through. Remove from the heat.

4. To assemble, lay the salad leaves on a serving plate and tip over the lentil mixture. Top with the grilled, sliced halloumi, torn fresh mint and chilli. Scatter over the chopped pecans and drizzle over the tahini sauce.

Note
· Store in the fridge for up to 3 days in an airtight container, keeping the dressing separate.

Griddled courgette, pea and pesto pasta salad

SERVES	TIME TO MAKE	SUITABLE FOR
4	30 MINS	V

This fresh-tasting pasta salad mixes griddled courgettes with fresh, sweet peas and a simple, homemade pesto. Most shop-bought pesto contains lower-quality ingredients such as canola oil, fewer pine nuts and less Parmesan, so making your own is worth the extra effort.

250g fusilli pasta (or any other short pasta)
120g frozen peas
1 courgette, sliced diagonally in 1cm coins
1 tbsp olive oil
Juice of 1 lemon
1 tbsp grated Parmesan cheese
Salt and freshly ground black pepper
Basil and mint leaves, to garnish

FOR THE PESTO
100g pine nuts
60g basil leaves
2 garlic cloves
60g Parmesan cheese, grated, plus extra shavings made with a vegetable peeler to garnish
1 tsp salt
8 tbsp olive oil

Notes
· Basil bruises easily, so only 'pulse' in the food processor to avoid ending up with a black pesto.
· Swap pine nuts for walnuts, cashews, almonds or Brazil nuts.
· Keep fresh pesto in the fridge for up to 5 days, or freeze in individual tubs or ice-cube trays with 1 teaspoon olive oil over the top to seal.

1. Start with the pesto. Toast the pine nuts in a dry frying pan for 5–10 minutes over a medium heat until toasted and golden, stirring constantly to make sure they don't burn (this happens very quickly). Remove from the heat and tip on to a clean plate in a single layer. Leave to cool completely or they will turn into a nut-butter paste when you blitz them. (Alternatively you could just use raw, untoasted pine nuts.)

2. Put the pine nuts, basil, garlic, Parmesan and salt into a food processor. Pulse a few times to bring it together, then gradually add the olive oil and pulse again until you reach your desired consistency. Taste and add more salt if necessary.

3. Bring a large saucepan of salted water to the boil. Add the pasta and cook for 1 minute less than packet instructions. For the last 2 minutes, tip in the frozen peas. Drain, reserving a few tablespoons of starchy pasta water. Run the pasta under cold water to stop it sticking and set aside.

4. Toss the sliced courgette in a bowl with the olive oil and a teaspoon of salt. Place a griddle pan over a high heat and sauté the courgette slices for 2–3 minutes on each side, until char lines appear, working in batches if needed.

5. Mix the charred courgettes in with the cooked pasta and peas. Spoon over half of the pesto, the lemon juice and the starchy pasta water to loosen. Mix everything together and season to taste. Finish with grated Parmesan, some freshly ground black pepper and a few basil and mint leaves.

SLOW, NOURISHING &
COMFORTING

SLOW, NOURISHING & COMFORTING

Shining a light on how we want to feel after we've eaten, this chapter is filled with comfort classics such as mac and cheese, roast chicken and risotto. Emotional eating is often described as a negative behaviour, but one of the best things about food is that it can provide real comfort and a sense of nourishment – both for the body and the soul.

That doesn't mean eating gallons of ice cream in one go, saying fuck it and ordering another takeaway or using emotional setbacks in life as excuses to self-sabotage. Popular romcoms have built upon this message to make us feel emotionally dependent on, or even judged by, our food choices: heartbroken woman cries into a family-sized chocolate bar. Same woman has an epiphany to change her life, loses weight, has coffee for breakfast, eats only salad and falls in love with the man of her dreams. This narrative could fit hundreds of movies and often makes us feel bad about when we do choose to enjoy ice cream, a takeaway or something that's not branded as 'healthy'.

'Don't let the fear of the time it will take to accomplish something stand in the way of doing it. The time will pass anyway.'

Mac and cheese after a long winter walk, mum's lasagne or the smell of a roast chicken filling the kitchen – for me these are all positive emotional memories tied to food and, just like a certain smell or photography, can remind me of some treasured times. Yet often, when we let ourselves live fully in the moment to enjoy simple pleasures such as food, we end up stuffing ourselves with way too much garlic bread, feeling guilty and then swearing to never let bread cross the doorstop again. This not only leads to a more black-and-white, good-and-bad way of thinking, one that has been shown to negatively impact the relationship we have with ourselves, but it's not sustainable and robs joy from the pleasure food can bring.

When I think of slow, nourishing and comforting foods I think of feeling warm, safe and comforted on a cold evening, enjoying delicious food from brightly coloured plates. Take the time to sit down and really enjoy them.

Mac and 3 cheese
Classic Bolognese
Lentil ragu
Lasagne 2 ways
Lemon, garlic and rosemary roast chicken
Mushroom and thyme risotto
Chicken shawarma flatbreads
Roast leg of lamb with Hasselback potatoes

Mac and 3 cheese

SERVES | TIME TO MAKE | SUITABLE FOR
6–8 | ⏱ 45 MINS | Ⓥ ❄

Comfort food at its best. I've used three different types of cheese here to add lots of flavour. A touch of Dijon mustard adds a subtle but fiery kick and the grilled breadcrumb topping adds a deliciously golden crunch to the creamy, cheesy filling underneath.

600g elbow macaroni pasta
120g butter, plus 2 tbsp
2 garlic cloves, very finely
   chopped
90g plain flour
1 litre whole milk
2 tbsp Dijon mustard
400g strong Cheddar cheese,
   grated
200g Gruyère cheese, grated
120g Parmesan cheese, grated
120g panko breadcrumbs
Salt and freshly ground black
   pepper
Chopped parsley, to garnish

1. Preheat the oven to 200°C/180°C fan and grease a large ovenproof dish (mine was 33 x 23cm).

2. Bring a large saucepan of salted water to the boil and cook the pasta for 2 minutes less than stated on the packet. Drain, then drizzle and toss with a little olive oil to keep from sticking together.

3. Melt the 120g butter in a large saucepan over a medium heat, add the garlic and stir for about a minute until aromatic. Add the flour and gently combine with a balloon whisk until the mixture looks like wet sand. Cook for about 1 minute, whisking all the time, then gradually pour in the milk, whisking until you have a smooth sauce. Simmer for 5–7 minutes (keep whisking) until thick and velvety, similar to condensed milk. Remove from the heat, stir through the mustard and season.

4. Stir through two-thirds of the grated cheeses, adding a handful at a time and stirring to mix together. Tip the drained, cooked pasta into the saucepan (or mix both in a large bowl), season with salt and pepper to taste and then pour the pasta mix into the greased baking dish.

5. Melt the 2 tablespoons butter in a small saucepan over a medium heat and add the breadcrumbs, stirring to coat. Cook for a couple of minutes until golden and crisp.

6. Scatter the remaining cheese over the pasta mix, followed by the breadcrumbs. Bake for 20–25 minutes until golden and crisp. I like to put this under a very hot grill for the last few minutes, so that the top of the macaroni has a golden, crunchy crust. Let it stand for 15 minutes before serving, scattered with parsley.

Notes
· This can be made in advance and kept in the fridge for up to 2 days before baking, or frozen for up to 3 months. Defrost overnight in the fridge before baking.
· Use any cheeses you love or stick to one or two types.
· Store leftovers in the fridge for up to 3 days.

Classic Bolognese

SERVES | TIME TO MAKE | SUITABLE FOR
6 | 30 MINS

An absolute classic and perfect for batch-cooking, this Bolognese can be ready within 30 minutes, or left to gently simmer away for up to 3 hours for a richer, deeper flavour. Pancetta adds a smoky flavour to a thick, velvety sauce that clings to the pasta – no watery puddles left here. This is the most popular savoury recipe from my website.

2 tbsp olive oil
150g pancetta, diced
1 onion, diced
4 garlic cloves, crushed
2 bay leaves
800g beef mince
125ml wine (red or white, see Notes)
4 tbsp tomato purée
1 beef stock gel/cube
2 x 400g tins chopped tomatoes
1 tbsp sugar (any, I use brown)
1 tbsp Worcestershire sauce
Salt and freshly ground black pepper

1. Place a large, heavy-based saucepan over a medium-high heat and add the olive oil. Once the oil is hot, add the diced pancetta and cook for 4–5 minutes until it just begins to colour. Add the onion, garlic, bay leaves and a pinch of salt. Cook over a medium heat for 8–10 minutes until the onion is soft and translucent.

2. Add the beef mince and use a wooden spoon to break it up, cooking until all the meat has browned and is no longer pink. Continue to cook until any excess water has boiled off, then add the wine and cook for a few more minutes until it's mostly evaporated.

3. Add the tomato purée and beef stock gel/cube, crumbling with your fingers if you're using a stock cube. Pour in both tins of tomatoes and fill one tin up with water – add this too. Finally, add the sugar, Worcestershire sauce and a pinch of salt and give everything a good stir. Bring to the boil and then reduce to a simmer.

TO SERVE
Pasta (I like tagliatelle or
    pappardelle)
Grated Parmesan cheese
Basil leaves

4. Let the Bolognese cook, with the lid off, for at least 20 minutes if you're pushed for time, and up to 3 hours for a rich, deep flavour and thicker sauce. Taste and adjust the seasoning (see Notes) as necessary.

5. To serve with pasta, boil the pasta according to the packet instructions and then drain, reserving a few tablespoons of the starchy pasta water. Mix the Bolognese in with the pasta, adding a little of the reserved pasta water to loosen the sauce, if needed. I always do it this way (rather than piling the sauce on top of the pasta) as it helps the sauce cling to the pasta. Serve with Parmesan, freshly torn basil and a grind of black pepper. A simple rocket and Parmesan salad is a good accompaniment.

Notes
- *To up the veg content, finely dice carrots, celery, mushrooms, etc. and add them at the end of step 1. Sauté for a few minutes until they begin to soften and then add the beef.*
- *You don't need to add the wine if you prefer not to, but if you do open a bottle, use one you'd be happy to drink the rest of by itself.*
- *Taste for seasoning at the end – I find that tomato-based dishes always need more seasoning than usual.*

Lentil ragu

SERVES | TIME TO MAKE | SUITABLE FOR

6 | **1 HR** |

I wanted to recreate a vegan ragu with the same texture and profile as a classic Bolognese without using meat substitutes so I'm really excited to share this recipe, packed with vegetables, protein, fibre and flavour. A thick, rich and slowly simmered sauce, the texture is meaty and wholesome. I've used finely chopped mushrooms, walnuts and lentils here alongside classic ragu vegetables and herbs.

300g dried red lentils
2 tbsp olive oil
1 brown onion, diced
2 carrots, diced
1 celery stick, diced
300g mushrooms, finely diced
4 garlic cloves, finely chopped
150ml red wine
800ml vegetable stock
30g walnuts, very finely chopped
400g tin chopped tomatoes
150g tomato purée
2 tsp dried oregano
2 tsp dried thyme
4 bay leaves
1 tbsp maple syrup
Salt and freshly ground black
    pepper

1. Soak the lentils in enough cold water to cover them while you prepare the vegetables – this reduces the cooking time.

2. Heat the oil in a large saucepan and sauté the onion over a medium heat for 5 minutes until soft. Add the carrots, celery and mushrooms and continue to cook for 10 minutes until the mushrooms have released their water, shrunk in size and turned golden. Stir through the garlic, add the wine and simmer until liquid has evaporated and the mixture is jammy, about 5 minutes

3. Pour in the stock, then add the drained lentils, walnuts, chopped tomatoes, tomato purée and herbs.

4. Bring to a simmer then cook over a medium heat at a gentle simmer for 40 minutes until the lentils are tender and saucy – top up with more water if needed. Season to taste with salt and pepper, then remove from heat and leave to cool slightly. Stir through the maple syrup and taste and adjust the seasoning as necessary.

Notes
· You don't need to add the wine if you prefer not to, but if you do open a bottle, use one you'd be happy to drink the rest of by itself.
· Check for seasoning at the end – I find tomato-based dishes need more seasoning than others.
· Store in the fridge for up to 5 days or freeze for up to 3 months. Use as a base for cottage pie, pasta bakes, lasagne, in tacos, piled on to nachos or on a jacket potato.

Lasagne 2 ways

SERVES | **TIME TO MAKE** | **SUITABLE FOR**
6-8 | 🕐 1 HR | ❄ Ⓥ

Using a batch of classic Bolognese (see page 80) or Lentil ragu (see page 82), here are two different ways to make a wholesome, comforting lasagne. The classic way uses a béchamel sauce which requires a few more ingredients and patience. The quick way uses ricotta cheese. Both result in a creamy, comforting dish layered with deep, rich sauce.

CLASSIC LASAGNE

1 batch of lentil ragu or classic
   Bolognese (see pages 80-2)
400g dried lasagne sheets
100g cheese (I use Cheddar and
   Parmesan), grated
Olive oil, for greasing
Chopped parsley, to serve

FOR THE BÉCHAMEL SAUCE
750ml whole milk
1 bay leaf
4 tbsp butter
60g plain flour
240g cheese (I use Cheddar and
   Gruyère), grated
¼ tsp grated nutmeg
Salt and freshly ground black
   pepper

1. To make the sauce, pour the milk into a small saucepan, add the bay leaf and warm over a low-medium heat.

2. Melt the butter in a large saucepan over a low-medium heat, then add the flour and use a balloon whisk to mix constantly until it's absorbed the butter and you have a sticky paste. Gradually pour in half the milk, discarding the bay leaf, while continuing to mix until smooth and there are no lumps. Pour in the remaining milk and continue to whisk. Bring the heat up slightly to a gentle simmer, continuing to whisk until the sauce has thickened and coats the back of a spoon, about 5 minutes. Remove from the heat, add the grated cheese, nutmeg and a generous pinch of salt.

3. To assemble the lasagne, grease a large, rectangular ovenproof dish (mine was 35 x 20cm) with olive oil and preheat the oven to 200°C/180°C fan.

4. Spread a third of the Bolognese or ragu into the base of the dish, top with lasagne sheets and spoon over a third of the béchamel sauce. Repeat the layers twice more. Top with the extra 100g grated cheese and bake for 40-45 minutes until the top is bubbling. I like to put this under a very hot grill for the last 5 minutes so that it forms a really crispy, golden brown crust. Remove from the heat and let it sit for 10-15 minutes before serving, scattered with chopped parsley.

QUICK LASAGNE

1 batch of lentil ragu or classic
   Bolognese (see pages 80–2)
400g dried lasagne sheets
100g cheese (I use Cheddar and
   Parmesan), grated
Olive oil, for greasing
Chopped parsley, to serve

FOR THE QUICK RICOTTA SAUCE
400g ricotta cheese
180g cheese (I use Cheddar and
   Gruyère), grated
1 large egg
¼ tsp grated nutmeg
Salt and freshly ground black
   pepper

1. In a bowl, mix together the ricotta, grated cheese, egg and nutmeg. Season with salt and pepper.

2. To assemble the lasagne, grease a large, rectangular ovenproof dish (mine was 35 x 20cm) with olive oil and preheat the oven to 200°C/180°C fan.

3. Spread a third of the Bolognese or ragu into the base of an ovenproof dish, top with lasagne sheets and spread over a third of the ricotta mix. Repeat the layers twice more. Top with the extra 100g grated cheese and bake for 40–45 minutes until the top is bubbling. I like to put this on under a hot grill for the last 5 minutes so that it forms a really crispy, golden brown crust. Remove from the heat and let it sit for 10–15 minutes before serving, scattered with chopped parsley.

Lemon, garlic and rosemary roast chicken

SERVES | **TIME TO MAKE** | **SUITABLE FOR**
4–6 | **1 HR 30 MINS** | **GF**

If you've never cooked a roast chicken before, now is the time to give it a go! Here, I've focused on classic and simple flavours that do all the work for you. Just a little preparation and you're left with a beautifully browned, crispy-skinned roast chicken in a puddle of buttery, garlic juice. Serve with your choice of sides (see pages 98–116).

1.5–2kg whole chicken
4 tbsp softened butter
20g rosemary, leaves picked and
    finely chopped
2 garlic cloves, crushed
2 unwaxed lemons
1 whole garlic bulb
Salt and freshly ground black
    pepper

1. Preheat the oven to 220°C/200°C fan.

2. Put the chicken on a chopping board and pat dry with kitchen paper; removing any excess moisture will help give it a really crispy, golden skin. Season every surface of the chicken, inside and out with lots of salt and pepper.

3. Make a herby baste by mixing the butter with most of the chopped rosemary, the crushed garlic cloves and the grated zest of 1 of the lemons. Gently lift the skin away from the breast of the chicken and press three-quarters of the butter paste underneath the skin on both sides, easing it in with your fingers. Rub any remaining butter all over the outside of the chicken.

4. Push 1 whole lemon (the one with the zest still on) inside the cavity of the chicken. Cut the other lemon in half and remove any seeds. Slice the whole garlic bulb in half horizontally. Place the chicken in a large, ovenproof skillet and tuck the halved lemon and halved garlic bulb around the chicken. Scatter with the remaining rosemary.

5. Roast for 50 minutes–1 hour 10 minutes, depending on size. To check for doneness, use a sharp knife to shred some of the meat along the thigh bone – the meat should look white and opaque and the juices run clear.

6. Let the chicken rest in the skillet for at least 15 minutes before carving with a sharp knife. Pour the buttery pan juices over the top of the meat and serve with the roasted lemon and garlic alongside.

Notes
· Use a snug-fitting skillet or any ovenproof roasting dish.
· Shred any leftover chicken from the carcass and store in an airtight container in the fridge for up to 5 days.
· You can also use a medium-sized roasting tin; just make sure the chicken fits snugly inside.

Mushroom and thyme risotto

SERVES | TIME TO MAKE | SUITABLE FOR
4 | ⏱ **30** MINS | **V** **GF**

Loaded with buttery garlic mushrooms on a pile of super-creamy risotto, this is my favourite go-to one-pan risotto dish. Made with just a handful of ingredients, I created this recipe while travelling New Zealand's beautiful South Island and cooking in a campervan (minimal equipment needed!).

5 tbsp butter

2 tsp thyme leaves

600g mushrooms (I use a mix of oyster, shiitake and Swiss brown), roughly sliced

3 garlic cloves, very finely chopped or grated

4 shallots, finely diced

250g arborio rice

120ml dry white wine (I use a sauvignon blanc)

1 vegetable stock cube

1.2 litres boiling water

100g Parmesan cheese, grated or shaved

Salt and freshly ground black pepper

Chopped chives or parsley, to garnish

1. Heat 3 tablespoons of the butter in a saucepan over a medium heat; once melted, add the thyme and mushrooms and a pinch of salt to season. Cook for 3–4 minutes until the mushrooms have softened and are starting to turn golden brown.

2. Stir the garlic through the mushrooms and cook for another 1–2 minutes until the garlic begins to turn golden, then remove the pan from the heat.

3. Tip the mushrooms into a bowl and set aside while you cook the risotto. If using the same pan, give it a quick wipe with a kitchen towel and return to the heat.

4. Melt the remaining 2 tablespoons butter over a low-medium heat. Once melted, add the shallots and cook until they have softened and are translucent (we want to keep them soft and not let them get crispy).

5. Add the arborio rice and stir constantly for about 1 minute until the rice turns from a bright white to translucent. Pour in the white wine to deglaze the pan, then simmer until most of the liquid has evaporated.

6. Dissolve the stock cube in the boiling water, then add about a quarter of this stock to the pan. Still over a medium heat, allow the mixture to come to a soft simmer. You don't need to constantly stir the risotto but the water will begin to absorb over the next 3–4 minutes and you don't want it to dry out or it will catch on the bottom of the pan, so stir occasionally to check.

7. Once the first batch of stock has mostly absorbed, add another quarter and repeat the simmer-until-mostly-absorbed steps until all of the liquid has been poured in, continuing to stir occasionally over a gentle simmer.

8. Continue to cook until most the of the stock is absorbed. The rice should be cooked but still al dente and with a creamy texture. You know it's ready when you mix the risotto with the back of a spoon, it should leave a clean 'path' on the bottom of the pan before slowly refilling, rather than pooling with liquid. (I prefer a thick and creamy risotto over a thinner, watery one.)

9. Once cooked to your liking, add about three-quarters of the mushrooms and most of the Parmesan, stirring briefly over the heat to warm through. Season to taste with salt and pepper.

10. Garnish with remaining mushrooms, Parmesan cheese and any fresh chopped herbs.

Chicken shawarma flatbreads

SERVES	HANDS-ON	HANDS-OFF
4	**20** MINS	**3** HRS +

A great meal to share! Prepare the chicken marinade and tahini yoghurt in advance so that all you have to do is bake the chicken and set the table. Put everything in separate bowls in the middle and let everyone help themselves, piling flatbreads high with the Middle Eastern spiced chicken, herbs, tahini yoghurt sauce and rocket.

8 chicken thigh fillets
2 tbsp olive oil

FOR THE MARINADE
1 tbsp ground coriander
1 tbsp ground cumin
2 tsp smoked paprika
1 tsp ground cardamom
2 garlic cloves, very finely
   chopped
2 tsp salt
Freshly ground black pepper
Juice of 1 lemon
4 tbsp olive oil

FOR THE TAHINI YOGHURT SAUCE
6 tbsp natural yoghurt
Juice of 1 lime
8 tbsp tahini
2 garlic cloves, crushed
Handful of chopped parsley
   (leaves and stalks)

1. Start by making the marinade. Dry-fry the spices over a high heat until aromatic, then tip into a bowl and allow to cool. Add the remaining marinade ingredients and mix together.

2. Use kitchen paper to pat the chicken thighs dry all over and then add to the bowl of marinade (or tip everything into a large ziplock bag). Use your hands to massage the spices into the thighs. Leave to marinate for at least 3 hours, or overnight

3. Combine all the tahini sauce ingredients in a small bowl with 2 tablespoons water, adding a little more water to thin if needed. Cover and chill in the fridge (up to 3 days in advance) until ready to serve.

4. Preheat the oven to 200°C/180°C fan. Place a large ovenproof frying pan or griddle pan over a high heat and add the olive oil. When hot, add the chicken pieces and cook until charred on the outside (you may need to do this in batches). Return all the chicken back to the pan and transfer to the oven for 6–8 minutes until cooked through.

Note
· Store any leftover chicken in the
  fridge for up to 3 days.
· Use gluten free flatbreads to make
  it GF.

TO SERVE

4 large (or 8 small) flatbreads
4 handfuls of rocket
Handful of mixed coriander, mint
  and parsley leaves
Sliced red onion
Pomegranate seeds

5. Remove the chicken from the oven, wrap in foil and allow to rest for 5 minutes, before thinly slicing the chicken with a sharp knife. Drizzle any juices remaining in the pan over the meat.

6. Sprinkle the flatbreads with water and pop them in the oven for 3–5 minutes to warm up. Meanwhile, combine the rocket and herbs in a bowl.

7. Put everything on the table so people can help themselves; I like to spread tahini sauce on to a flatbread, then top with chicken, rocket and herbs, sliced red onion and a sprinkle of pomegranate seeds.

Roast leg of lamb with Hasselback potatoes

SERVES | **TIME TO MAKE** | **SUITABLE FOR**
6 | 🕐 **2 HRS** | **GF** **DF**

One-pan roasts are easy to assemble, easy to wash up and so much easier than they look to cook. This is a super-simple and very tasty way to cook a leg of lamb and delicious hasselback potatoes all in one roasting tin.

2kg leg of lamb (bone-in)
1kg white potatoes
1 tbsp olive oil
1 tsp good-quality sea salt
Few sprigs of rosemary
1 whole garlic bulb, halved horizontally

FOR THE RUB
4 garlic cloves
1 tbsp olive oil
3 sprigs of rosemary, leaves picked
4 sprigs of thyme, leaves picked
1 tbsp wholegrain mustard
1 tbsp good-quality sea salt
Freshly ground black pepper

1. Remove the lamb from the fridge one hour before roasting so that it can come to room temperature while you prepare the potatoes and the herb rub.

2. The easiest way to make Hasselback potatoes is to push a metal or wooden skewer through the potato lengthways, just off centre. Use a sharp knife to cut thin slices vertically all the way across the potato, about 3mm apart, slicing down to the skewer (the skewer will stop the knife sliding right the way through). Remove the skewer once sliced and repeat until all of the potatoes have been sliced.

3. Put the potatoes in a bowl with the olive oil and sea salt and use your hands to rub all over the potatoes.

4. For the rub, place all the ingredients into a small food processor and whizz to combine, or finely chop everything, add to a small bowl and mix into a paste.

5. Preheat the oven to 210°C/190°C fan. Pat the leg of lamb dry with a kitchen paper and use a sharp knife to score the top of the lamb leg in diagonal lines, about 3cm deep and 3cm apart. Put the lamb in the centre of a large, deep roasting tin, scored side up, and use the back of a spoon to spread the herb rub all over the lamb, pushing it into the scored fat.

6. Surround the lamb with the Hasselback potatoes, sliced sides up, then add the rosemary sprigs and halved garlic bulb. Roast in the oven for 1 hour 40 minutes (different sized cuts may require different timings) removing once or twice to baste the meat and potatoes with the juices from the lamb (remember to shut the oven door while you do this to prevent the heat escaping). If you like your lamb more well done, roast for an extra 20 minutes.

7. Once the lamb has cooked to your liking, remove the roasting tin from the oven and lift out the lamb, leaving it to rest on the side for at least 15 minutes, wrapped loosely with foil to keep warm. Return the potatoes to the oven to crisp up if needed.

8. Once rested, remove potatoes from the oven and carve the lamb into slices, following the bone. Serve with the Hasselback potatoes and whatever accompaniments you prefer, such as a mint or redcurrant jelly or gravy and steamed spring greens.

CENTRE-STAGE SIDE DISHES

CENTRE-STAGE SIDE DISHES

Side dishes are too often skimmed over in our meals, but I really believe that it's the small touches that make the biggest difference. When I'm having friends or family over, I like to put all the food in separate serving bowls so everyone can help themselves.

This not only makes it easier for people to build their own plate based on hunger and taste preferences, but the whole 'can you please pass me the ...' chatter that follows really does add to the shared enjoyment and sense of community.

These recipes are also great for those occasions when you need to 'bring a dish' but are not sure what to bring. Nobody ever spends much time on the sides, so you can guarantee yours will stand out. Using a handful of extra ingredients (usually already hiding in our cupboards) such as soy sauce or tamari, miso, honey and garlic, we can inject so much flavour into these dishes. Small details and finishing touches come together to really bring vegetables to life.

'You can't use up creativity. The more you use, the more you have.'

Say no to boring overboiled or unseasoned steamed vegetables and add these small touches to simple dishes to keep your meals interesting and flavoursome.

Miso, chilli and lime-buttered corn on the cob

Hasselback roasted butternut squash with honey, feta and pecans

Potatoes 3 ways

Ratatouille

Tomato, burrata and basil salad with crispy garlic, shallots and balsamic vinaigrette

Garlic and Parmesan roasted vegetables

Red cabbage and apple slaw with a lime, honey and jalapeño dressing

Charred tenderstem broccoli with chilli, ginger and sesame

Green beans with flaked almonds and crispy shallots

Crispy Yorkshire puddings with a garlic and sage butter

Miso, chilli and lime-buttered corn on the cob

SERVES | **TIME TO MAKE** | **SUITABLE FOR**
6 | 🕐 **25 MINS** | Ⓥ ⒼⒻ

This side dish is inspired by one of my favourite restaurants in Cheltenham, Bao & BBQ, where fiery Texan grill meets Taiwanese cuisine. They use miso in both their savoury and sweet dishes, giving them a gorgeous umami flavour. I love making extra miso, chilli and lime butter and using it to brighten up other vegetables too. It's been requested so often that I regularly make big batches of it and roll it up in a butter log to gift. It's perfect for barbecues too!

6 whole corn cobs
60g butter
40g miso paste (see Note)
Zest and juice of 2 limes
1 red chilli, deseeded and finely
    chopped
2 tbsp vegetable oil
Handful of chopped parsley
Grated Parmesan cheese, to serve

1. Bring a large saucepan of salted water to the boil. Add the corn cobs and cook at a gentle roiling boil for 10 minutes. Drain and set to aside.

2. Mix the butter and miso paste together in a small bowl until smooth and even in colour. Mix in half the lime zest and all of the chilli.

3. Preheat a griddle pan or large frying pan over a high heat. Pat the drained cobs dry and brush all over with the oil. Add to the hot pan and cook for 6–10 minutes, turning every few minutes until golden and charred.

4. Remove the cobs from the pan and brush each one all over with the miso butter. Sprinkle with the rest of the lime zest, the parsley and the grated Parmesan. Squeeze over the lime juice, then serve.

Note
· Miso paste is usually gluten free but do check the label.

Hasselback roasted butternut squash with honey, feta and pecans

SERVES | **TIME TO MAKE** | **SUITABLE FOR**
6-8 | 🕐 1 HR 20 MINS | Ⓥ Ⓖ🅕

Impressive enough to be a centrepiece by itself, sweet roasted butternut squash is finished with salty feta, roasted pecans and sticky honey. Hasselback butternut squash creates a stunning side dish and is hearty enough to serve as a vegetarian main dish.

2 butternut squash
8 tbsp olive oil
4 sprigs of thyme, leaves stripped
6 tbsp honey, plus extra for
  drizzling
60g pecans
120g feta
Salt and freshly ground black
  pepper
Chopped fresh parsley, to garnish

1. Preheat the oven to 240°C/220°C fan.

2. Peel the butternut squash with a vegetable peeler, then slice in half lengthways and use a spoon to scoop out and discard the seeds and pulp.

3. Rub ½ tablespoon olive oil over each squash half and place them cut side down in a roasting tin. Season with salt and roast in the oven for 20 minutes, then set aside until cool enough to handle.

4. Place the handle of a wooden spoon on either side of a roasted squash half – these will act as a 'stopper' when slicing into the squash as you don't want to slice all the way through. Use a sharp knife to slice down into 3mm slices, stopping when the knife blade touches the wooden handles. Repeat for the remaining squash halves.

5. Drizzle the remaining 6 tablespoons olive oil and the thyme leaves over the squash halves and roast, sliced sides up, for 20 minutes.

6. Remove from the oven, drizzle over the honey and scatter over the pecans, then return to the oven for another 20 minutes. Crumble over the feta while the squashes are still hot, finishing with another drizzle of honey, some black pepper and the chopped parsley.

Potatoes 3 ways

SERVES | **TIME TO MAKE**
6-8 | ⏱ **25** MINS

One of the most versatile vegetables, here are 3 of my favourite ways to enjoy potatoes.

THE BEST CRISPY HOMEMADE CHIPS

TIME TO MAKE | **SUITABLE FOR**
⏱ **1** HR | VE

2kg floury potatoes (Maris Piper, King Edward or Russet), peeled
2 tbsp malt or white vinegar
2 tsp salt
8 tbsp sunflower or groundnut oil
4 tsp cornflour

1. Preheat the oven to 220°C/200°C fan. Trim the rounded sides of each potato to make a rectangular block, then cut into thick batons. Rinse in a large colander under cold running water, then tip into a large saucepan, cover with cold water and add the vinegar and salt. Bring to the boil, then reduce the heat slightly and cook for 8 minutes until tender when pricked with a fork but still firm.

2. Meanwhile, add the oil to a large roasting tin and put into the oven to heat up.

3. Drain the potatoes and lay out on a clean tea towel to absorb any excess water. Pat dry and place in a large bowl, then sprinkle over the cornflour and use clean hands to gently toss them, being careful not to break them.

4. Carefully tip the potatoes into the hot oil, gently turning to coat them, then arrange in a single layer. Bake for 40 minutes, turning the chips over halfway through.

PARMESAN AND POLENTA CRISP ROASTED POTATOES

TIME TO MAKE | SUITABLE FOR
🕐 **50 MINS** | **GF**

2kg floury potatoes, peeled and quartered
2 tsp salt
180g duck fat
120g polenta
60g Parmesan cheese, finely grated
8 garlic cloves, crushed
2 tbsp finely chopped rosemary
2 tbsp salt

1. Preheat the oven to 220°C/200°C fan.

2. Place the potatoes in a large saucepan of cold water with the 2 teaspoons salt. Bring to the boil, then reduce the heat and boil gently for 8 minutes. Drain in a large colander and shake to roughen the edges up.

3. Meanwhile, put the duck fat into a large roasting tin and put into the oven to heat up.

4. Add the polenta and Parmesan to a small bowl and mix together. Tip one third of the potatoes back into the saucepan and add a third of the coating. Put the lid on the saucepan and shake to mix, then tip the potatoes into the tin of hot duck fat and turn to coat them. Repeat twice more, until they are all evenly coated. Scatter over the garlic, rosemary and sea salt and roast for 20–25 minutes, turning halfway through until golden brown.

CRUSHED GARLIC AND ROSEMARY NEW POTATOES

TIME TO MAKE | SUITABLE FOR
🕐 **35 MINS** | **VE** **GF**

2kg new potatoes
120ml olive oil
8 garlic cloves, crushed
8 sprigs of rosemary, leaves chopped
Salt and freshly ground black pepper

1. Preheat the oven to 200°C/180°C fan.

2. Put the potatoes into a large saucepan, cover with cold water and add 1 teaspoon salt. Bring to the boil, then reduce to a rolling boil and cook for about 10 minutes until tender when pricked with a fork but still firm. Drain and leave to cool a little.

3. Mix olive oil, garlic and chopped rosemary together in a small bowl.

4. Tip the drained potatoes into a large roasting tin and toss with the herby oil using your hands. Use a masher to press down and roughly crush the potatoes until their interiors are exposed. Season with salt and pepper and then roast in the oven for 20–25 minutes.

Ratatouille

SERVES | TIME TO MAKE | SUITABLE FOR
6   50 MINS

Packed with roasted vegetables, this ratatouille uses a splash of balsamic vinegar to add a deeper flavour. It's a great stand-alone dish to dunk with sourdough, stir through pasta or as a delicious side. I always have a few portions stashed away in my freezer to defrost and warm up after a heavy weekend when I need lots of vegetables!

1 aubergine, cubed

2 courgettes, cubed

2 tbsp olive oil, plus extra for drizzling

1 tbsp dried thyme (or use fresh leaves)

2 tbsp olive oil

1 yellow onion

2 garlic cloves, chopped

2 peppers (I use 1 red, 1 yellow), diced

2 x 400g tins chopped tomatoes

2 tbsp tomato purée

1 tbsp balsamic vinegar

1 tsp sugar

Handful of basil leaves

Salt and freshly ground black pepper

1. Preheat the oven to 220°C/200°C fan.

2. Evenly spread out the cubed aubergine and courgette on a baking tray. Drizzle with olive oil, sprinkle over the thyme and add a generous pinch of salt. Roast in the oven for 30 minutes.

3. Meanwhile, heat the 2 tablespoons olive oil in a heavy-based saucepan over a medium heat and add the onion, garlic and peppers. Cook for about 10 minutes, stirring often, until softened and the onion is translucent. Remove from the heat and set aside until the vegetables in the oven have finished roasting.

4. Once roasted, add the aubergine and courgette to the pan along with the chopped tomatoes, tomato purée and a generous pinch of salt. Bring to the boil, then reduce to a simmer and cook for 30 minutes with the lid on.

5. Remove from the heat, stir in balsamic vinegar and sugar and tear in the basil leaves. Stir to combine then taste and adjust the seasoning.

Note
· To store, allow to cool to room temperature, then transfer to an airtight container. Keep in the fridge for up to 5 days or in the freezer for up to 6 months.

Tomato and burrata salad with crispy garlic, shallots and balsamic vinaigrette

SERVES **6-8** | TIME TO MAKE **15 MINS** | SUITABLE FOR **V** **GF**

Simple and oh so special, this takes a caprese salad to another level with the crispy garlic and shallots adding lots of flavour and texture. For best results, always make sure your tomatoes are at room temperature, and buy them on the vine if possible; for an aesthetic twist, look out for orange, yellow or green striped heirloom ones.

2 tbsp olive oil
2 garlic cloves, thinly sliced
1 shallot, thinly sliced
6 large tomatoes, thinly sliced
Handful of basil leaves
300g (2 large balls) burrata
Salt and freshly ground black
   pepper

FOR THE DRESSING
4 tbsp olive oil
2 tbsp aged balsamic vinegar
½ tsp dried oregano

1. First make the dressing: whisk the olive oil and vinegar together with a fork in a small bowl. Rub the oregano between your fingers to release the oils and sprinkle into the oil and vinegar. Season with salt and pepper and set aside.

2. Place a large frying pan over a medium heat and add the olive oil; once hot, add the sliced garlic. Sauté until golden, then use a slotted spoon to transfer to a separate plate. Repeat with the shallot, frying until just golden. Pour any of the remaining olive oil into the dressing – it will be bursting with flavour.

3. Arrange the sliced tomatoes on a large serving plate, tear over the basil leaves and sprinkle generously with salt. Tear the burrata over and scatter over the crispy garlic and shallots. Pour the dressing over the top and serve immediately.

Garlic and Parmesan roasted vegetables

SERVES | TIME TO MAKE | SUITABLE FOR
8 |  50 MINS | V GF

Using a mandoline to slice vegetables thinly and uniformly is a really quick and easy way to make simple dishes look impressive. Tossed in olive oil and drizzled with garlicky butter and Parmesan before roasting – this comes together really quickly and is an impressive addition to any dinner table. Use any root vegetable; I like golden or pink beetroots but you could also use any potatoes, turnips or carrots. Just make sure that your slices are as even in size and thickness as possible.

4 tbsp butter, plus extra for greasing
3 orange sweet potatoes
2 purple sweet potatoes
4 raw beetroots
6 tbsp olive oil
2 tsp salt
8 garlic cloves, crushed
2 tsp fresh thyme leaves
6 tbsp finely grated Parmesan cheese
Salt and freshly ground black pepper

1. Preheat the oven to 220°C/200°C fan and grease a baking dish with butter (I use a 26 x 21cm oval baking dish).

2. Prepare your vegetables, slicing into thin even circles; if you are using a mandoline, set the blade to 2mm and be very careful. If you don't have a mandoline, use a sharp knife to slice as evenly and thinly as you can.

3. Mix the oil and salt together in a large bowl, then add the sliced vegetables and use your hands to toss them, evenly coating them so that they don't dry out in the oven. If you're using beetroot, do this in a separate bowl to avoid the colour bleeding into the other vegetables and use food-safe gloves to prevent pink hands for the next few days! Once finished, layer the vegetables in the dish in a spiral pattern, working from the outside in. I use 4 or 5 slices of each vegetable, alternating colours. Don't worry about keeping it perfect, it looks (and tastes!) just as good rustic-style. Keep any smaller circles for the centre.

4. Melt the butter with the garlic and thyme in a small saucepan over a low heat. Pour this over the vegetables and use the back of a metal spoon to push the garlic and thyme into the cracks and evenly across the vegetables.

5. Sprinkle the top with grated Parmesan and some salt and pepper, then bake in the oven for 35–40 minutes until the edges of the vegetables are golden and crisp.

Red cabbage and apple slaw with a lime, honey and jalapeño dressing

SERVES | **TIME TO MAKE** | **SUITABLE FOR**
4-6 | 🕐 **15 MINS** | **V** **GF**

I've used natural yoghurt and lime here for a light, tangy dressing. Mixed with fresh herbs, a touch of sweet honey and with a kick from the jalapeño, this is a bright and refreshing side dish that can also be used to stuff into burgers, pittas or hot-dog buns.

6 tbsp natural yoghurt
2 tbsp honey
Zest and juice of 2 limes
½ red cabbage, finely chopped
2 Granny Smith apples, cut into
    matchsticks
2 spring onions, finely chopped on
    the diagonal
Small bunch of coriander,
    chopped
Small bunch of mint, chopped
1 jalapeño pepper, deseeded and
    finely chopped
Salt and freshly ground black
    pepper

1. Put the yoghurt, honey, lime zest and juice and some salt and pepper in a small bowl whisk together with a fork until combined.

2. Tip the sliced cabbage, apples, spring onions, herbs and chopped jalapeño into a large bowl and use clean hands to toss together. Pour over the dressing and mix well.

Notes
· To make this vegan, use a dairy-free yoghurt, such as soya or coconut yoghurt and use maple syrup
*   in place of the honey.*
· Make this up to 2 days ahead and store in the fridge in an airtight container.

Charred tenderstem broccoli with chilli, ginger and sesame

SERVES | **TIME TO MAKE** | **SUITABLE FOR**
6-8 | 🕐 **10** MINS | VE GF

Vibrant green, crispy and bursting with flavour, this popular Chinese side dish uses garlic, ginger and chilli to transform simple vegetables into taste sensations. Broccoli is blanched first and then stir-fried to char the outside, keep its bite firm, lock in nutrients and keep it vibrant in colour. This is worlds away from soggy, bland, overboiled vegetables. Taking only a few minutes to come together, this uses mostly storecupboard essentials for a quick, ready-to-go side dish.

800g tenderstem broccoli
4 tbsp groundnut oil
6 garlic cloves, crushed
Thumb-sized piece of fresh ginger, peeled and grated
2 tsp chilli flakes
2 tbsp tamari
2 tbsp sesame seeds
2 spring onions, sliced diagonally

1. Use a sharp knife to trim the broccoli, cutting any thick bits of stalk in half.

2. Bring a saucepan of salted water to the boil and blanch the broccoli for 2–3 minutes, then drain.

3. Heat the oil in a griddle pan or wok over a high heat. Add the garlic, ginger and chilli flakes and sauté for about 30 seconds. Add the drained broccoli and the tamari and stir-fry for another minute.

4. Remove from the heat, scatter over the sesame seeds and sliced spring onions and serve immediately.

Green beans with flaked almonds and crispy shallots

SERVES
6–8

TIME TO MAKE
🕐 **10 MINS**

SUITABLE FOR
VE **GF**

Blanched and then stir-fried, fresh green beans paired with crispy flaked almonds and fried shallots make this a super-simple side dish to pull together.

700g green beans, trimmed
60g flaked almonds
3 tbsp olive oil
4 shallots, diced
4 garlic cloves, finely chopped
Juice of 1 lemon
Salt and freshly ground black
  pepper

1. Bring a saucepan of water to the boil and blanch the beans for 4 minutes until bright green and tender but still with some bite.

2. Toast the almonds in a dry frying pan or wok until golden. Remove from the heat and wipe any crumbs from the pan.

3. Heat the olive oil in the same pan over a high heat, then fry the shallots until crispy. Throw in the green beans and garlic and sauté for 2 minutes until charred.

4. Remove from the heat and transfer a serving plate. Season with salt and pepper, squeeze over the lemon juice and scatter over the toasted flaked almonds.

Crispy Yorkshire puddings with a garlic and sage butter

SERVES | TIME TO MAKE
6 | 50 MINS

An essential side to any roast, these are deceptively simple. My tips for the best sky-high Yorkshire puddings is to have really hot fat in the roasting tin, allow the batter to thicken and cool in the fridge beforehand and avoid any heat escaping the oven. It's the cold–hot shock that will cause your Yorkshires to rise and crisp up on the outside. The type of fat matters too; I prefer beef dripping or (for vegetarians) vegetable oil. I use a deep 6-hole jumbo muffin tin, or you could make 12 regular-sized puddings.

140g plain flour
4 eggs, beaten
200ml milk
6–12 tsp beef dripping (or vegetable oil)
Salt and freshly ground black pepper

FOR THE GARLIC AND SAGE BUTTER
150g butter, at room temperature
4 garlic, very finely chopped
10 sage leaves, finely chopped

Notes
· This butter is also amazing with any accompanying roasted vegetables
· Use vegetable oil to keep it vegetarian.

1. Tip the flour into a large measuring jug and make a well in the centre. Pour the beaten eggs into the flour and use a balloon whisk to mix everything together. Add the milk and whisk again (it's okay if it's a bit lumpy). Refrigerate for at least 30 minutes, or overnight.

2. Preheat the oven to 240°C/220°C fan. Spoon 1 teaspoon of beef dripping or vegetable oil into the base of each hole in the muffin tin and then put the tin into the preheated oven for 10–15 minutes to heat up the fat; it should be smoking. Remove the jug from the fridge, season with salt and pepper and give it another whisk.

3. Remove the hot tin carefully from the oven (closing the door) and pour the batter into the holes, filling them about two-thirds full. Put the tin back in the oven and close the door; don't open the door again until the puddings are risen, golden, crisp and cooked, about 16–18 minutes.

4. To make the garlic and sage butter, beat the butter, garlic and sage together in a small bowl and season with a good pinch of salt and pepper. Serve alongside the Yorkshires, to be dolloped on top of each pudding.

ANY EXCUSE
TO BAKE

ANY EXCUSE TO BAKE

I've always had a sweet tooth, so my favourite recipes to create and share are baked goods. I have very fond early memories of my sister and I having second servings and then finding that extra 'stomach' after a full Sunday roast to fit in my ultimate dessert: sticky toffee pudding and ice cream.

Cakes, traybakes and cookies were the first things I started experimenting with when I was learning to cook, and any celebration was an excuse to bake and practise new recipes, flavours or techniques.

As we move through life and become increasingly exposed to social media, our behaviour around food can start to be influenced as it often encourages dichotomous thinking: 'good' versus 'bad' foods, or the concept of 'treat' or 'cheat' foods, making it hard to enjoy eating or even creating delicious recipes without feelings of guilt. But the motto: 'everything in moderation, including moderation' is one that I love to live by. One of the best things that I did for my mental health was to choose the full-fat, full-sugar versions of foods that I loved; choosing real ice cream rather than the low-calorie alternatives that might leave me full – but not satiated. These are also marketed to us as one tub being one serving, often more deeply ingraining any negative eating behaviours. This mentality can lead us to continue to feel guilty and subsequently further restrict or remove the foods that brought true satisfaction. Give me one scoop of good-quality, full-fat ice cream over a tub of low-calorie, air-whipped alternative any day.

'Happiness comes from experiences, but fulfilment comes from giving.'

Knowing this, it brings me so much joy to bring you recipes packed with full-fat love. I really think that when we make the effort to make recipes from scratch, knowing what goes into them, spending time carefully mixing, measuring and baking them, the appreciation (and taste) we get from them is ten times that we'd get if we quickly picked something off the shelf. I'm a big fan of taking the time to sit down to eat as an opportunity to slow down and really enjoy and savour my food and the people around me. Life isn't perfect and of course that's not always possible – but what better way to pause the day than with a slab of cake and a hot coffee?

Cheesy garlic tear-and-share bread
Classic pork and sage sausage rolls
Spiced black bean, sweet potato and cheese rolls
Cranberry, pistachio and thyme seeded crackers
Fruit scones
Guinness chocolate brownies with a Bailey's buttercream frosting
Three-ginger loaf with lemon icing
Salted chocolate brownie cookies
Salted tahini, honey and chocolate chip cookies
Peanut butter, chocolate and pretzel no-churn ice cream
The ultimate Victoria sponge
Peach, honey and thyme tarts
Biscoff fudge
Baked figs in maple syrup with walnuts
Sticky toffee pudding with hot toffee sauce
New York baked cheesecake with miso caramel sauce

Cheesy garlic tear-and-share bread

SERVES	HANDS-ON	HANDS-OFF	SUITABLE FOR
8	⏱ **15** MINS	⏱ **2** HRS 15 MINS+	Ⓥ ❄

Put this in the middle of the table and it's every man and woman for themselves! Baked with two types of cheese, each buttery, gooey ball is stuffed with mozzarella, layered in Parmesan and wrapped in a herby, garlicky, buttery layer. Golden and crisp on the outside and baked in a Bundt tin, it looks stunning and leaves a circle in the centre – perfect for dips. Bread recipes take a bit more time from start to finish but this is really simple to create (most of the recipe time is allowing the dough to rise).

280ml tepid water
1 tbsp honey
7g fast-action dried yeast
450g strong white bread flour
60ml olive oil, plus extra for
    greasing
1 tsp salt
220g mozzarella (32 mini
    mozzarella pearls)
80g Parmesan cheese, grated
Flaky sea salt, to serve

FOR THE HERBY BUTTER
120g butter
2 garlic cloves, very finely
    chopped (or use 1 tsp garlic
    powder)
2 tsp dried Italian herb seasoning
1 tbsp finely chopped parsley

1. Mix the tepid water and honey together in a jug and then sprinkle the yeast over the water. Leave for 5 minutes until it's foamy.

2. Put the flour, olive oil and salt into a large bowl and mix together, then pour in the yeast mixture and use a spoon to bring everything together into a dough.

3. Use your hands to knead for 10–12 minutes (or use a stand mixer fitted with a dough hook for 8 minutes) until the dough is smooth and elastic. It should feel soft but shouldn't stick to your hands, so add a few extra tablespoons of flour if the dough is too wet.

4. Lightly grease a large clean bowl with olive oil and place the dough in it. Cover with cling film and leave in a warm spot to rise for 1 hour, or until the dough has doubled in size. Meanwhile, generously oil a 25cm Bundt tin.

5. Melt the butter in a small saucepan over a low heat and add the garlic and herbs. Let it simmer for a few minutes and then remove from the heat and set aside.

6. When the dough has risen, remove the cling film and punch the dough firmly once to release any air bubbles. Cut the dough in half, then in half again and continue dividing the dough until you have 32 balls. Wrap each piece of dough around a mozzarella pearl, pinching to seal.

Notes

· You can use chunks of Cheddar instead of mozzarella in this recipe, use rosemary for the herby butter, or flavour the bread with olives or sundried tomatoes.

· If you don't have a Bundt tin, any baking tin that keeps the balls snugly packed together will work.

· This bread can be made ahead and frozen: allow to cool completely, double-wrap in cling film and freeze for up to 3 months. Defrost before reheating in an oven preheated to 200°C/180°C fan for 10 minutes.

7. Dip each dough ball into the herby butter and place in the prepared Bundt tin. Build up layers of balls, sprinkling grated Parmesan over each layer and finally over the top. Keep any extra herby butter to one side.

8. Let the dough rise again in the Bundt tin for 45 minutes

9. Preheat the oven to 210°C/190°C fan and bake for 25–30 minutes until golden brown. Remove from the oven and leave to cool for 10 minutes in the tin before tipping upside down on to a serving plate to release the bread. Pour over the remaining herby butter (gently warm over a low heat if needed), sprinkle with flaky salt and serve warm.

Classic pork and sage sausage rolls

MAKES
24 | TIME TO MAKE
50 MINS | SUITABLE FOR

The perfect finger food, sausage rolls are absolutely delicious eaten warm, straight out the oven, or cold for a picnic or lunchbox snack. Here, all-butter flaky pastry is filled with juicy pork, sage, onion, bacon, garlic and a touch of wholegrain mustard for a subtle kick. Serve with a tomato sauce or my very favourite chilli and tomato relish.

2 x sheets all-butter ready-rolled puff pastry (I use 2 x 215g sheets)
1 egg
Nigella seeds (see Notes)
Sage leaves (optional)

FOR THE FILLING
1 tbsp olive oil
2 garlic cloves, finely chopped
1 onion, finely diced
200g streaky bacon (about 12 rashers), finely chopped
450g minced pork or sausage meat
60g panko (or regular) breadcrumbs
1 egg
2 tbsp wholegrain mustard
2 tbsp sage, finely chopped (about 16 leaves)
Salt and freshly ground black pepper

1. If you're using frozen pastry, ideally defrost overnight in the fridge (or at room temperature for about an hour). Don't unroll the sheets until you're ready to assemble the sausage rolls.

2. Heat the oil in a large non-stick frying pan over a medium heat and add the garlic, onion and a pinch of salt. Sauté until the onion is soft and translucent, but not coloured. Add the bacon and stir through until cooked; again, we're not looking for crispy bacon bits here, just cooked through. Remove from the heat and set aside to cool.

3. Put all the remaining filling ingredients in a large bowl and mix together. Use clean hands to make sure everything is well mixed through and then add the cooked garlic, onion and bacon mix, wiping the frying pan clean (you'll use this again in a little bit). Mix through with clean hands or using food-safe gloves.

4. Place the frying pan over a medium–high heat and pinch off a small ball of the mixture. Add to the pan and fry for a few minutes until cooked. Taste for seasoning – I usually find it needs a little more salt and pepper at this stage. Adjust the seasoning if necessary and repeat the frying and tasting until you are happy.

5. Prepare your egg wash by beating the egg in a small bowl. Unroll your pastry sheets, keeping them on their baking paper, and use a sharp knife to cut each one in half lengthways, so you end up with 4 long strips in total.

- *If you don't have time to chill the sausage rolls before baking, give them a quick 10-minute flash freeze instead; this helps to firm up the dough for easier slicing and means you can squeeze the pastry gently round the meat, which will stop the filling falling out.*
- *Use poppy seeds or white or black sesame seeds instead of nigella seeds.*
- *The unbaked sausage rolls can be kept for up to 3 days in an airtight container in the fridge, or frozen for up to 3 months. To bake from frozen, simply add the eggwash and seeds as above and add 10 minutes to the baking time.*

6. Scoop out a quarter of the mixture and lay it in the centre of one pastry strip. Egg wash one long side of the pastry and then fold over the other side. Use your hands to gently squeeze and encompass the filling; the egg wash should help the pastry stick together like a licked envelope. Pinch together at the seam with your fingers. Repeat this until all 4 strips have been filled. Refrigerate for at least 30 minutes (see Notes), saving the remaining egg wash for later.

7. When you're ready to bake them, preheat the oven to 200°C/180°C fan and remove the sausage rolls from the fridge. Use your hands to firmly squeeze along the sausage rolls so that they're nice and tight (see Notes). Flip them over so they are seam side down and use the remaining egg wash to brush them all over. Top with nigella seeds and sage leaves (if using) and then use a sharp knife to slice each roll into 4cm pieces.

8. Bake for 30–35 minutes until golden. Serve with a fresh watercress salad and tomato dipping sauce.

Spiced black bean, sweet potato and cheese rolls

MAKES | TIME TO MAKE | SUITABLE FOR

24 | **50 MINS** |

I love creating vegetarian alternatives and using a variety of spices and herbs to make them exciting. This one is loaded with fibre and flavour and is layered with spices, textures and colour.

2 x sheets all-butter ready-rolled puff pastry (I use 2 x 215g sheets)
1 egg
Nigella seeds (see Notes)
Sage leaves (optional)

FOR THE FILLING
1 sweet potato, peeled and cubed (about 250g)
2 tbsp olive oil
2 garlic cloves, finely chopped
1 onion, finely diced
2 tsp smoked paprika
1 tsp ground cumin
1 tsp ground coriander
400g tin black beans, drained and rinsed
60g panko (or regular) breadcrumbs
120g Cheddar cheese, grated
2 tsp fresh thyme
Handful of parsley, roughly chopped (stalks and leaves)
Zest of 1 lemon
Salt and freshly ground black pepper

1. If you're using frozen pastry, ideally defrost overnight in the fridge (or at room temperature for about an hour). Don't unroll the sheets until you're ready to assemble the rolls. Preheat the oven to 220°C/200°C fan.

2. Spread the cubed sweet potato out on a baking tray and drizzle with 1 tablespoon olive oil. Bake for 20–25 minutes, or until tender. Remove from the oven and set aside.

3. Heat the remaining tablespoon of oil in a large non-stick frying pan over a medium heat and add the garlic, onion and a pinch of salt. Sauté until the onion is soft and translucent, but not coloured. Turn the heat to low and add the paprika, cumin and coriander, stirring to mix. Remove from the heat and set aside.

4. Tip the roasted sweet potato into a large bowl and add the black beans, breadcrumbs, grated cheese, herbs and lemon zest. Use a potato masher or fork to very roughly mash, leaving some whole beans and sweet potato chunks. Use clean hands to make sure everything is well mixed through and then add the cooked garlic, onion and spices. Taste for seasoning. I usually find it needs a little more salt and black pepper at this stage. Adjust recipe if necessary and taste again until you're happy.

5. Prepare your egg wash by beating the egg in a small bowl. Unroll your pastry sheets, keeping them on the baking paper, and use a sharp knife to cut each in half lengthways, so you end up with 4 long strips in total.

6. Scoop out a quarter of the mixture and lay it in the centre of one pastry strip. Egg wash one long side of the pastry and then fold over the other side. Use your hands to gently squeeze and encompass the filling; the egg wash should help the pastry stick together like a licked envelope. Pinch together at the seam with your fingers. Repeat this until all 4 strips have been filled. Refrigerate for at least 30 minutes (see Notes), saving the remaining egg wash for later.

7. When you're ready to bake them, preheat the oven to 200°C/180°C fan and remove the rolls from the fridge. Use your hands to firmly squeeze along the rolls so that they're nice and tight (see Notes). Flip them over so they are seam side down and use the remaining egg wash to brush them all over. Top with nigella seeds and sage leaves (if using) and then use a sharp knife to slice each roll into 4cm pieces.

8. Bake for 20–25 minutes until golden. Serve with a fresh watercress salad and tomato dipping sauce.

Cranberry, pistachio and thyme seeded crackers

MAKES	HANDS-ON	HANDS-OFF	SUITABLE FOR
40	🕐 15 MINS	🕐 3 HRS 15 HRS	Ⓥ ❄

150g plain flour
30g rolled oats
80g cranberries
60g unshelled pistachio nuts
30g sunflower seeds
30g flaxseeds
50g soft light brown sugar
1 tsp bicarbonate of soda
1 tsp salt
2 tsp dried thyme
½ tsp ground cinnamon
250ml milk (or more if needed)

Notes
· *Use a small loaf tin for small, snappable crackers.*
· *Once twice-baked these will keep for up to 1 month in an airtight container.*
· *Swap the nuts, seeds and spices used here for your own favourites: try pumpkin seeds, walnuts, or chopped rosemary. Just keep the ingredient weights the same.*
· *To make these vegan, use a dairy-free milk alternative.*

For me the perfect sharing board includes cheese, crackers, fruit, olives and prosciutto. These are like gourmet biscuits – only better. They are super-versatile too – try mixing your own seeds and nuts depending on what you have in the cupboard. These are twice-baked, the second time from frozen but before slicing (this makes it much easier to slice them into thin crisps). This is an ideal recipe to stash in the freezer after its first bake for those occasions when one wine turns into a few, lunch rolls into dinner and you need something to eat. Once twice-baked and sliced, they last for several weeks.

1. Preheat the oven to 200°C/180°C fan and grease and line a loaf tin with baking paper.

2. In a large bowl, put the flour, oats, cranberries, nuts, sunflower seeds and flaxseeds into a large bowl and mix with clean dry hands to break up any cranberries or nuts stuck together. Add the sugar, bicarbonate of soda, salt, thyme and cinnamon and mix again. Pour in the milk and stir to a thick batter, adding a little more liquid if needed.

3. Pour the batter into the prepared loaf tin and bake for 30 minutes until golden brown and a skewer comes out clean. Remove from the oven and leave in the tin to cool completely. Remove from the tin and wrap in cling film, then transfer to the freezer for 2 hours (or up to 3 months).

4. When you are ready to bake, remove the loaf from the freezer and allow to defrost for about 20 minutes while you preheat the oven to 140°C/120°C fan.

5. Use a sharp serrated knife to cut the loaf into 3mm thick slices and arrange in a single layer across 2 baking sheets. Bake for 45 minutes until golden, turning halfway through. Transfer to a wire rack to cool completely; they will harden to give a 'snap' when you break them.

Fruit scones

MAKES | TIME TO MAKE | SUITABLE FOR
8 | 50 MINS | ❄ Ⓥ

Warm, crumbly scones, studded with juicy sultanas and served with clotted cream and (for me) raspberry jam, are a true British delight. The key to foolproof scones is to handle the dough as little as possible and to keep all the ingredients cold. The method is simple and these can be frozen ahead of time (and baked from frozen), meaning that if you have last-minute visitors, you can always whip up an impressive afternoon tea in no time.

120g sultanas
175ml whole milk
2 eggs
1 tsp vanilla bean paste (or use vanilla extract)
380g self-raising flour, plus extra for dusting
1 tsp baking powder
½ tsp salt
40g caster sugar
90g cold butter, cubed

1. Put the sultanas into a small bowl, cover with boiling water and set aside for a few minutes; this plumps them up and stops them from burning.

2. Whisk together the milk, 1 egg and the vanilla in a jug with a fork.

3. Sift the flour, baking powder and salt into a large bowl, then add the sugar and stir to mix.

4. Add the cubed butter to the flour and use your fingertips to rub into the flour mixture (or pulse in a food processor) until it resembles breadcrumbs. If rubbing by hand, make sure you work with cold hands (rinse them under a cold tap and then dry) and handle the ingredients as little as possible. Make a well in the centre of the mix and pour in the whisked wet ingredients. Drain the sultanas, discarding any excess water, then use a spoon to bring everything together into a dough.

5. Grease and line a baking tray and set aside. Lightly dust a work surface with flour and tip out the dough. Avoid heavy handling (or kneading) of the dough; use your hands to pat it out into a rectangle, roughly 4cm thick. Dip the scone cutter into flour, then cut rounds pushing the cutter straight down (don't twist it into the dough). Place each scone upside down on the baking tray (to get a nice flat top on it). Reshape any leftover dough and continue cutting until it is all used. You should get 8 large scones.

Notes

- These are best served on the day you bake them but they will keep in an airtight container for up to 3 days.
- Soak the sultanas in fruit juice – or try brandy or rum – for 3–24 hours. Try grating in orange for citrus-zest twist.
- These can be frozen before baking for up to 3 months and you don't need to defrost them before baking – simply add 8–10 minutes to the baking time.

6. Chill the scones on the baking tray in the fridge for 30 minutes (this isn't essential but really helps them keep their shape). Meanwhile, preheat the oven to 220°C/200°C fan.

7. Beat the remaining egg and use a pastry brush to glaze the top of the scones. Try not to let any drip down the sides of the scones, as this can affect the rise.

8. Bake for 15 minutes until risen, golden brown and they sound hollow when tapped with a wooden spoon.

9. Move to a wire rack to cool for a few minutes, before slicing in half and serving with clotted cream and your favourite jam or preserve.

Guinness chocolate brownies with a Baileys buttercream frosting

MAKES | **TIME TO MAKE** | **SUITABLE FOR**
16 | **1** HR |

With a malty sweetness and deep, luxurious colour, Guinness (much like coffee) is the perfect addition to the rich and slightly bitter chocolate in brownies. The Guinness is gently simmered down to a reduction that locks in all of the flavour notes and baked in with the brownie batter. The baked brownie is topped with a delicious, velvety buttercream with the boozy tang of Baileys. This is for my Irish friends who treat me like family.

440ml Guinness
180g unsalted butter
210g dark chocolate (70% cocoa solids)
120g plain flour
1 tsp salt
240g caster sugar
1 tsp vanilla bean paste (or use vanilla extract)
3 large eggs

FOR THE BAILEYS BUTTERCREAM
160g unsalted butter
420g icing sugar
Pinch of salt
½ tsp vanilla bean paste (or use vanilla extract)
120ml Baileys

Notes
· If you don't want to use Guinness, swap with 120ml freshly brewed coffee.
· Store for up to 3 days in the fridge. Unfrosted brownies can be frozen after baking and cooling – wrap tightly in cling film and freeze for up to 3 months.

1. Pour the Guinness into a saucepan, place over a medium heat and simmer for 20 minutes until reduced by three-quarters. Pour into a heatproof bowl and set aside. Preheat the oven to 200°C/180°C fan and grease and line a 20cm square baking tin with baking paper.

2. Using the same saucepan, gently melt the butter and dark chocolate together over a low heat, stirring to mix. Remove from the heat when they are almost melted as they will continue to melt together off the heat.

3. Mix the flour, salt and sugar in a large bowl. Add the vanilla, then mix in the eggs, one at a time, to combine. Pour in the melted butter and chocolate, with the reduced Guinness, folding together until just mixed.

5. Pour into the prepared tin and bake for 30 minutes – it's okay if the middle is still jiggly as the brownies will continue to cook out of the oven. Cool completely.

6. For the buttercream, use a hand-held electric whisk to beat the butter for a few minutes until light and fluffy. Add the icing sugar, a little at a time, and whisk on a medium–high until all the sugar has been added. Add the salt and vanilla, then gradually add the Baileys until the consistency is soft but stable, like toothpaste. Spoon or pipe on to the cooled brownies. Best served chilled, so keep in the fridge and remove 30 minutes before serving.

Three-ginger loaf with lemon icing

SERVES	TIME TO MAKE	SUITABLE FOR
12	🕐 **1 HR**	

Intense, squidgy and loaded with spices and three types of ginger. Black treacle gives this bake a deep flavour and dark brown colour. Although this is perfectly sticky and sweet by itself, I love the combination of lemon and ginger so I top it with a lemon icing to cut through the intense ginger.

120g unsalted butter
140g black treacle
120g golden syrup
220g plain flour
½ tsp bicarbonate of soda
100g soft dark brown sugar
1 tsp mixed spice
1 tsp ground cinnamon
1 tbsp ground ginger
Pinch of salt
2 large eggs
100ml whole milk
4 balls of stem ginger, finely
    chopped
Sliced crystallised ginger and
    grated lemon zest, to decorate

FOR THE LEMON ICING
120g icing sugar
Juice of 1 lemon
2 tbsp syrup from the stem
    ginger jar

1. Preheat the oven to 200°C/180°C fan and grease and line a 900g (2lb) loaf tin with baking paper.

2. Put the butter, black treacle and golden syrup into a small saucepan and gently melt together over a low heat. Remove from the heat as soon as the butter has melted down and leave to cool slightly.

3. Sift the flour and bicarbonate of soda into a large bowl and stir in the sugar, ground spices and salt. Make a well in the centre and crack in the eggs, one at a time, followed by the milk. Stir to roughly mix. Pour in the melted butter mixture and chopped ginger and mix until it's all come together.

4. Pour into the prepared loaf tin and then bake for 40–45 minutes until a skewer inserted into the centre comes out clean. Leave to cool for 10 minutes in the tin before transferring to a wire rack to cool completely.

5. Meanwhile make the icing: sift the icing sugar into a bowl, add the lemon juice and ginger syrup and mix until smooth, thick and glossy. Pour over the cake, spreading with the back of a spoon so that it drips slightly over the sides. Scatter over the crystallised ginger and lemon zest, then leave to set.

Notes
· The flavours develop and intensify over the first few days, so this is a great option to make ahead.
· Store for up to 5 days in an airtight container at room temperature.
· You can freeze the cake before icing: wrap tightly in cling film and then foil and freeze for up to 3 months.

Salted chocolate brownie cookies

MAKES **TIME TO MAKE** **SUITABLE FOR**
12 ⏱ **30 MINS** ❄ Ⓥ

With the signature brownie 'crackle' on top and a rich, fudgy texture inside, these double chocolate cookies are studded with extra chocolate chips finished off with a sprinkle of sea salt to cut through the sweetness. They taste absolutely incredible, it's hard to believe they're so easy to make.

60g unsalted butter
220g dark chocolate (70% cocoa solids)
100g plain flour
10g cocoa powder
1 tsp baking powder
½ tsp salt
2 large eggs
90g caster sugar
90g soft light brown sugar
1 tsp vanilla bean paste (or use vanilla extract)
100g chocolate chips
Flaky sea salt, to decorate

1. Preheat the oven to 195°C/175°C fan and line 2 baking trays with baking paper.

2. Melt the butter and chocolate together in a saucepan (or in a heatproof bowl in the microwave) until it's three-quarters melted. Remove from the heat (it will continue to melt).

3. Sift the flour, cocoa powder, baking powder and salt into a bowl and mix to combine.

4. In a separate bowl, mix the eggs, both sugars and the vanilla together with a hand-held electric whisk on high speed for about 2 minutes, or until frothy and doubled in volume.

5. Turn the electric whisk to low and pour in the melted and slightly cooled chocolate and butter mixture; continue to whisk on low until combined.

6. Add the flour mixture to the bowl and fold through with a spatula – the mixture should be heavy, glossy and thick. Finally, add the chocolate chips and fold through.

7. Use a spoon to scoop out the batter (1 heaped tablespoon per cookie) and use your hands to roll into a ball. Place on the baking tray and gently press down just a little. Keep the cookies 5cm apart (they will spread in the oven) on the baking tray and bake for 12 minutes until the tops are shiny, set and have the distinctive brownie 'crackle' on top. Remove from the oven and as soon as they have firmed up enough, move them to a wire rack.

8. Sprinkle with a pinch of flaky sea salt to finish.

Notes
· Use dark, milk or white chocolate chips – or a combination!
· Make sure your eggs are at room temperature before you start.
· Keep in an airtight container for up to 5 days. The unbaked dough balls can be frozen for up to 3 months; bake from frozen for 15–18 minutes

Salted tahini, honey and chocolate chip cookies

MAKES	HANDS-ON	HANDS-OFF	SUITABLE FOR
12	15 MINS	2 HRS 15 HRS	

Strong and earthy tahini paired with sweet honey and chocolate chips make for a very moreish batch of cookies. My first experience of tahini in a sweet bake was in Bali, where they'd serve little tahini cookies to dip in your coffee. Tahini, made from ground sesame seeds, is a great alternative to nut butter. I make these ahead and freeze in little balls so that there's always something ready to bake in the freezer when guests come over or just when I fancy one!

140g plain flour
½ tsp baking powder
½ tsp bicarbonate of soda
1 tsp flaky sea salt, plus extra for sprinkling
120g butter
130g tahini
2 tbsp honey
80g soft light brown sugar
100g caster sugar
1 large egg
1 tsp vanilla bean paste (or use vanilla extract)
200g chocolate chips

Notes
· These can be baked straight from the freezer – chilling the dough (often called 'hydrating') allows the butter and fats to solidify; when placed in a hot oven, they melt more slowly, resulting in thicker, chewier cookies that are evenly bronzed – not flat, sad and thin discs!
· If you're short on time you can just flash-freeze for 20–30 minutes – it really makes a difference so is definitely worth doing!

1. Line a baking sheet with baking paper.

2. Mix the flour, baking powder, bicarbonate of soda and salt in a large bowl and set aside.

3. Put the butter into another large bowl and use a hand-held electric whisk to whip it for a few minutes until pale and fluffy. Add the tahini, honey and both sugars and beat on a medium speed. Add the egg and vanilla and whisk again to combine.

4. Add the dry flour mixture to the wet and use a spatula or wooden spoon to fold until just combined. Add the chocolate chips and fold through again.

5. Use an ice-cream scoop to scoop out balls of the dough on to the prepared baking sheet. Repeat until you've used all the dough and then put into the freezer for 2 hours. After 2 hours the balls should be solid; you can then place them all in a ziplock bag and store them in the freezer until you're ready to bake.

6. Preheat the oven to 180°C/160°C fan and line a baking sheet with baking paper. Space the cookies 5cm apart (they will spread) and bake for about 15 minutes until golden around the edges. Don't worry if they still look unbaked in the middle as they'll continue to bake out of the oven. Sprinkle with flaky salt immediately.

Peanut butter, chocolate and pretzel no-churn ice cream

SERVES	HANDS-ON	HANDS-OFF	SUITABLE FOR
10	20 MINS	6 HRS+	

Ice cream is usually served on the side, but this chunky, packed ice cream is absolutely special enough to be the main attraction! Make ahead of time and stash in the freezer to always have something special for a dessert. Salty, sweet and each bite studded with chunks of flavour.

397g tin sweetened condensed milk
250g peanut butter
1 tsp vanilla bean paste (or use vanilla extract)
1 tsp salt
480ml double cream
100g peanut butter cups, roughly chopped
80g dark chocolate chunks
80g pretzels, roughly crushed
Flaked sea salt, for sprinkling

1. In a bowl, mix together the condensed milk with 125g of the peanut butter, the vanilla and salt. Put the remaining peanut butter into a small saucepan and melt gently over a low heat. Set aside.

2. In another bowl, use a hand-held electric whisk to whip the cream on high speed for about 3 minutes until stiff peaks form, stopping as soon as they do – you don't want to overbeat.

3. Use a rubber spatula to fold the condensed milk mixture into the cream and stir until mixed through.

4. Spoon one-third of the cream mixture into the base of a metal loaf tin and spread in an even layer. Top with 2 tablespoons of the melted peanut butter, a handful of chopped peanut butter cups, chocolate chunks and crushed pretzels. Use a knife to swirl through and then repeat the layers twice more, finishing the top layer with some extra whole chunks of peanut butter cups, pretzels, chocolate and a sprinkling of flaked sea salt.

5. Freeze for at least 6 hours before serving. After 6 hours, tightly wrap in cling film to avoid freezer burn.

Notes
· This will keep in the freezer for up to 3 months.
· Double cream can also be called 'heavy whipping cream'.
· Check the salt levels in your peanut butter; if it's already quite salty, you might not need the extra salt. I prefer using the cheaper supermarket own-brand peanut butter here but use whatever is your favourite!

The ultimate Victoria sponge

SERVES | **TIME TO MAKE** | **SUITABLE FOR**
12 | ⏱ **1 HR** |

This really is the ultimate Victoria sponge! Light and fluffy vanilla sponge is sandwiched together with thick buttercream, warmed strawberry jam and piles of fresh berries. It's one of the simplest recipes with classic ingredients and techniques but it really does look beautiful and impressive when decorated.

FOR THE SPONGE

220g self-raising flour

1½ tsp baking powder

½ tsp salt

220g unsalted butter, at room temperature

220g caster sugar

4 large eggs, at room temperature

2 tbsp milk

1 tsp vanilla bean paste (or use vanilla extract)

6 heaped tbsp strawberry or raspberry jam

Fresh berries and mint sprigs, to fill and decorate

1. Preheat the oven to 190°C/170°C fan and grease and line 2 x 20cm cake tins with baking paper.

2. Sift the flour, baking powder and salt into a bowl and stir to mix.

3. In a separate large bowl (or stand mixer fitted with the paddle attachment), beat the softened butter until smooth, then add the sugar and cream together until light and fluffy. Crack in the eggs one at a time, mixing well after each addition.

4. Tip the dry ingredients into the wet mixture and add the milk and vanilla. Gently fold until just combined.

5. Divide the cake batter between the 2 prepared tins and use the back of a metal spoon to smooth the surfaces. Bake on the middle shelf of the oven for about 20 minutes, or until golden. The sponges are ready when they have a soft spring back when gently pushed with fingertips and a metal knife or skewer comes out with no raw batter (a few crumbs are okay but you don't want wet streaks).

6. Leave the sponges in their tins until cool enough to touch, then transfer to a wire rack to cool completely. This cake is best assembled once it's completely cooled, otherwise the buttercream melts off!

FOR THE BUTTERCREAM
150g unsalted butter
300g icing sugar, sifted
1 tsp vanilla bean paste (or use
   vanilla extract)
1–2 tbsp milk
Pinch of salt

7. To make the buttercream, put the butter into a large bowl and use a hand-held electric whisk (or stand mixer fitted with the paddle attachment) to whip the butter until it's pale and fluffy. Gradually add the sifted icing sugar and continue to beat on a low speed until smooth. Add the vanilla and milk a tablespoon at a time, or just enough to loosen the mixture, and mix until smooth.

8. Once the sponges have completely cooled, warm the jam in a small saucepan over a low heat. Remove from the heat once it's warmed through (this just helps you to pour it evenly over – it doesn't need to be hot).

9. To assemble the cake, spoon one-third of the buttercream on top of one sponge. Pile on a single layer of fresh berries and press them down to 'glue' them to the buttercream. Pour the warmed jam over the berries. Spoon the remaining buttercream frosting on top of the second sponge and sandwich it on top. Decorate the top with fresh berries, starting with the big ones first and filling in the gaps with smaller ones and mint leaves.

Peach, honey and thyme tarts

 SERVES
6

 TIME TO MAKE
40 MINS

 SUITABLE FOR
V

I love the combination of warm fruit with honey and thyme, especially on top of flaky, buttery pastry brushed with vanilla-infused cream cheese. This is an easy, throw-together dessert and you can use whatever fruits need using up, although you can't beat a delicious peach when they're in season.

375g ready-rolled puff pastry sheet
180g cream cheese
4 tbsp icing sugar
1 tsp vanilla bean paste (or use vanilla extract)
3 peaches, halved, stoned and sliced into thin wedges
3 tbsp brown sugar
1 egg, beaten
Honey, for drizzling
Fresh thyme leaves
Icing sugar, to serve

1. If you are using frozen pastry, defrost overnight in the fridge or at room temperature for about an hour. Don't unroll it until all of your toppings are ready. Preheat the oven to 240°C/220°C fan.

2. Unroll the puff pastry on to a large baking sheet lined with non-stick baking paper. Use a sharp knife to slice the sheet into 6 even rectangles, then score a border (about a finger width) around the edges of each piece of pastry. This will puff up into a beautiful, flaky crust.

3. Put the cream cheese into a bowl and use a hand-held electric whisk to beat until smooth. Add the icing sugar and vanilla and beat again until combined. Use a spoon to spread this mixture on to each tartlet, avoiding the border you have scored. Top each one with wedges of peach and sprinkle over the brown sugar.

4. Use a pastry brush to brush the borders with the beaten egg; this gives the pastry a shiny, golden finish. Bake for 20–25 minutes, or until the pastry is crisp and golden and the base is cooked.

5. Once baked, remove from the oven then generously drizzle with honey and sprinkle with thyme leaves. Just before serving, finish with a dusting of icing sugar.

Note
· *Other fruits (plums, apricots, nectarines) also work really well here.*

Biscoff fudge

MAKES	HANDS-ON	HANDS-OFF	SUITABLE FOR
64 SQUARES	⏱ **15** MINS	⏱ **3** HRS +	**V**

No oven, no thermometer and only a handful of ingredients. This is a super-simple fudge recipe that's perfect for those with an insatiate sweet tooth (like me!). Wrap them individually in baking paper or food-safe wrap, secure with string or twine or pack them neatly into a gift box.

6 Biscoff biscuits
300g good-quality white chocolate
397g tin condensed milk
1 jar Biscoff spread (I use crunchy but smooth would work too)

1. Grease and line a 20cm square cake tin with baking paper.

2. Put the biscuits into a ziplock bag and crush with your hands or by lightly bashing with a rolling pin. Set aside (you'll use these for the topping later).

3. Put the white chocolate and condensed milk into a saucepan and melt together over a low–medium heat. Remove from the heat once it's completely melted and add two-thirds of the Biscoff spread. Stir to mix this in, returning to a low heat if you need help melting it all down.

4. Pour the mixture into the lined tin and even out with the back of a spoon.

5. Warm the remaining Biscoff spread over a low heat and pour this on top of the mix, then press the crumb mixture on top.

6. Leave to set in the fridge for at least 3 hours until completely firm and cooled. Remove from the tin and use a sharp knife to cut into 2.5cm squares.

Baked figs in maple syrup with walnuts

SERVES	TIME TO MAKE	SUITABLE FOR
6	🕐 **25** MINS	VE GF

Sweet, earthy and packed with nutrients, figs release their delicious juices when baked. They should be perfectly ripe when picked as they don't continue to ripen (unlike avocados or bananas) so make sure you're happy with the ones you bring home. Add to ice cream, yoghurt, cheeseboards, pancakes or toast, or enjoy by themselves for a sweet, sticky dessert.

12 ripe figs (Black Mission or Turkish are my favourite varieties)
8 tbsp maple syrup
1 tsp fresh thyme leaves
Pinch of salt
80g walnut halves
Pinch of ground cinnamon (optional)

1. Preheat the oven to 220°C/200°C fan and line a baking tray with baking paper.

2. Slice the figs in half and add to a bowl with the maple syrup. Use your hands to gently toss to coat in the syrup, then sprinkle with the thyme and salt.

3. Tip into a small roasting tin and bake for 20 minutes until the figs are soft and the juices are running and bubbling. Remove from the oven and set aside to cool a little (the sauce will thicken as it cools).

4. Serve the figs with the sauce spooned over and topped with the walnuts and a dusting of cinnamon, if using.

Note
· Cool and store in the fridge in an airtight container for up to 3 days.

Sticky toffee pudding with hot toffee sauce

SERVES | TIME TO MAKE | SUITABLE FOR
12 |  1 HR 10 MINS |

My all-time favourite dessert has to be sticky toffee pudding. If it's on the menu, I'll always make room. A soft, lightly spiced sponge studded with dates and enough warm toffee sauce to sink a ship. Rich and indulgent, it's just the ultimate comfort food.

180g dates, pitted and roughly chopped
160ml boiling water
220g self-raising flour
1 tsp bicarbonate of soda
1 tsp baking powder
80g unsalted butter, softened
160g soft dark brown sugar
1 tsp vanilla extract
3 tbsp black treacle
2 large eggs
100ml whole milk
Good-quality vanilla or toffee ice cream, to serve

FOR THE TOFFEE SAUCE
120g unsalted butter
240g light brown sugar
200ml double cream
1 tbsp black treacle
Pinch of salt

Notes
· Store the sponge in an airtight container for up to 5 days; keep the sauce separate. Freeze the sponge, wrapped in cling film then foil, for up to 3 months. Defrost before using.
· Add 120g roughly chopped pecans.
· For a boozy twist, add up to 60ml brandy or rum to the toffee sauce.

1. First, put the dates in a large bowl and cover with the boiling water. Leave for 30 minutes to soften. Use the back of a fork to mash together roughly.

2. Preheat the oven to 200°C/180°C fan and grease and line a 20cm ovenproof dish with butter.

3. Sift the flour, salt, bicarbonate of soda and baking powder together into a large bowl. Set aside.

4. In a separate bowl, cream the butter and sugar together. Add the vanilla and treacle and beat again to mix. Add in the eggs, one at a time, beating between.

5. Add the flour mixture into the wet ingredients and gently fold until just combined, being careful not to overmix. Add the milk and mashed date mixture, gradually, stirring until everything is mixed in; it will be a thin mixture but this is what we're looking for!

6. Pour the batter into the prepared baking dish and bake for 30–35 minutes, until a skewer comes out clean.

7. For the sauce, add all the ingredients to a large saucepan over a medium heat until melted together. Bring the sauce to a boil, then reduce to a simmer for a few minutes, stirring often, until thickened.

8. Remove the baked sticky toffee pudding and leave to cool slightly, then use a skewer to prick holes all over the sponge and pour over most of the toffee sauce, keeping some in a jug for people to help themselves to!

New York baked cheesecake with miso caramel sauce

SERVES | TIME TO MAKE | SUITABLE FOR
12 | ⏱ 1 HR+ | ❄   Ⓥ

A creamy, velvety baked vanilla cheesecake on a buttery biscuit base. This recipe requires a little more time but has no fancy or complicated bain-marie method and results in a delicious and smooth cheesecake – with no cracks on top! The miso caramel sauce brings salted caramel to a whole new level. I'm absolutely obsessed – and it offsets the perfectly smooth and velvety baked cheesecake.

FOR THE BASE
250g digestive biscuits
175g butter, melted
Pinch of salt

FOR THE FILLING
500g full-fat cream cheese, at room temperature
2 tbsp plain flour
350g caster sugar (I use 300g white, 50g golden)
150g sour cream
1 tsp vanilla bean paste (or use vanilla extract)
Zest of 1 lemon
3 large eggs, at room temperature

FOR THE TOPPING
140g caster sugar
120ml double cream
2 tsp white miso paste

1. Preheat the oven to 180°C/160°C fan. Grease and line the sides and base of a 20cm springform cake tin with baking paper.

2. For the base, use a food processor to blitz the biscuits to a sand-like consistency (or put into a ziplock bag and bash with a rolling pin). Combine with the melted butter and salt, then tip into the lined tin and press down firmly until there are no loose crumbs, making a small 1cm lip around the edges to create a crust for your cheesecake base. Chill in the fridge while you make the filling.

3. Put the cream cheese into a large bowl and beat with a hand-held electric mixer on medium speed for about 1 minute. Add the flour and beat again for a few seconds until combined. Add the sugar, sour cream, vanilla and lemon zest and mix together on medium speed for a few seconds until just mixed. Add the eggs one at a time, beating between each addition until each egg is mixed through.

4. Pour the filling into the prepared crust and bake for 50 minutes–1 hour on the middle shelf of the oven. Don't open the door for at least 50 minutes; the cheesecake will be ready when the top is golden brown and it has a slight jiggle in the centre.

5. Once ready, turn the oven off and open the oven door slightly. Allow the cheesecake to cool there for 2 hours, then remove from the oven and place in the fridge for another 2 hours, still in its tin.

6. Unclip the springform tin and remove any baking paper from the sides, then slide the cheesecake on to a flat surface.

7. For the topping, put the sugar and 4 tablespoons of water into a saucepan and place over a medium heat. Stir together and bring the mixture to a gentle simmer, being careful not to touch the liquid sugar. The sugar will start to caramelise and turn golden brown, at which stage remove from the heat and carefully pour in the cream while mixing with a balloon whisk. Whisk in the miso paste and set aside to cool (it will continue to thicken).

8. To serve, pour the warm but slightly cooled miso caramel over the cheesecake.

DRINKS

DRINKS

Long gone are the days of throwing back WKD Blues, vodka limes and bright purple pitchers of Cheeky WooWoos (if you know, you know). Or chugging back a smoothie or protein shake, one foot leaving the gym, one foot entering the office, while refreshing emails and checking social media.

Though I look back on those days with fond memories of equal parts ignorance and determination, nowadays I like my cocktails to carry more flavour and substance, while I prefer my smoothies to be enjoyable, not a bland scoop of protein powder, water and a frozen banana.

For gatherings and occasions where food isn't the main focus, drinks can still take centre stage with small and thoughtful touches, such as garnishes: think twists of orange peel, or ribbons of cucumber or rhubarb. For picnics, dates or packing to go, rather than carrying around several heavy clinking bottles, risking spillages, stains and mess, mix drinks into clean jam jars or have a pre-made mix ready to go (such as the margarita or bloody Mary mix). These also make a great gift, or are perfect for when you're not quite sure what to bring to the party.

'The glass is neither half empty nor half full – its refillable.'

These drinks are made to sip mindfully and enjoy slowly, either alone or in good company. Please choose to drink responsibly.

SMOOTHIES
Peanut butter and jelly smoothie
Piña colada smoothie
Cherry and almond smoothie
Blueberry, date and tahini smoothie
Green fresh smoothie
Warm coconut and chocolate malt smoothie

COCKTAILS
Cherry Negroni
Port and tonic (the new G&T)
Homemade limoncello
Bloody Mary
Homemade margarita mix
Rum-spiked hot chocolate

Peanut butter and jelly smoothie

SERVES | **TIME TO MAKE** | **SUITABLE FOR**

4 | ⏱ **10 MINS** |

Worth getting out of bed for, this is one of my favourite flavour combinations. I make the berry compote separately and usually double the batch so there's always some in the fridge – it's also delicious swirled through oats or yoghurt. Layered up in a glass, this looks beautiful and tastes much more like a dessert than breakfast.

FOR THE BERRY COMPOTE
200g strawberries
100g raspberries
1 tbsp maple syrup
1 tsp chia seeds

FOR THE SMOOTHIE BASE
2 bananas (fresh or frozen)
4 Medjool dates
4 tbsp peanut butter
500ml dairy-free milk
Pinch of salt
Handful of ice (if using fresh bananas)

1. For the compote, put the berries, 2 tablespoons water and the maple syrup into a small saucepan and place over a medium–high heat for about 5 minutes until bubbling and the berries have softened. Remove from the heat and use a masher or fork to roughly smash the berries. Add the chia seeds and stir through.

2. Put all of the smoothie base ingredients into a blender and whizz up, adding a handful of ice if you are using fresh bananas.

3. Spoon a heaped tablespoon of the berry compote into the bottom of each glass, using the back of the spoon to smear it up the sides. Pour in the smoothie mix and swirl a final teaspoon of compote through the top of the smoothie.

Notes
· *Keep the smoothie base and compote in separate containers in the fridge for up to 3 days, so you can put together whenever you're ready.*
· *Swap the peanut butter with any other nut butter you like, or mix up berries to use your favourites.*

Piña colada smoothie

SERVES | TIME TO MAKE | SUITABLE FOR
4 | 5 MINS | VE GF

Reminiscent of the beachy cocktail, this is super-thick and creamy, thanks to the yoghurt and frozen pineapple chunks. Using frozen fruit saves on time and mess and as they're prepared and frozen when they're ripe, it means you can still enjoy them when they're not in season. Sweet, satisfying and refreshing – this is summer personified. Add a shot of rum to make it boozy.

650g frozen pineapple (or use fresh)
400ml tin coconut milk
300g Greek yoghurt
2 tbsp honey
Pinch of salt
Handful of ice (if using fresh pineapple)
Fresh mint leaves and shredded coconut, to decorate

1. Put all of the ingredients, except the mint leaves and coconut, in a blender and whizz until smooth, adding a handful of ice for a thicker consistency if your pineapple isn't frozen.

2. Pour into glasses and top with fresh mint leaves and shredded coconut.

Notes
· *The mixture will keep in the fridge for up to 3 days.*
· *Tinned coconut milk is best here for a creamy consistency and intense flavour, but a good-quality coconut milk (the ones used as a milk alternative) will also work.*
· *To make this vegan, use a dairy-free yoghurt alternative and maple syrup instead of honey.*

Cherry and almond smoothie

SERVES | **TIME TO MAKE** | **SUITABLE FOR**
4 | 5 MINS | GF

This is such a refreshing, delicious smoothie! Sweet, tart cherries mixed with the nutty, smooth flavour of almonds gives a pleasing hint of cherry Bakewell – I finish it off with a squeeze of lime which really brings it to life. There are so many layers of flavour going on within one glass and I always make several servings so that I can have breakfast ready to go in the week. This is one of my favourites to start the day and packs over 16g of protein per serving without any added extras – just make sure you take 5 minutes to sip and savour it.

450g frozen pitted cherries
500ml coconut milk
250g Greek yoghurt (I use 5% fat)
4 tbsp almond butter
4 tbsp maple syrup
2 tsp almond extract
Pinch of salt
Handful of ice (optional)
Juice of 1 lime
Flaked almonds, to finish

1. Put all of the ingredients, except the lime juice and flaked almonds, in a blender and whizz until smooth. Use a handful of ice if your ingredients aren't frozen or chilled for a thicker consistency.

2. Once blended, squeeze in the lime juice and stir through. Pour into glasses and top with a sprinkle of flaked almonds.

Notes
- *This will keep for up to 3 days in the fridge. The ingredients may separate but that's absolutely fine – I just whizz mine up with a few ice cubes the next day to keep the thick consistency.*
- *You can use any type of milk, or coconut water works well too.*
- *Almond extract can be found by the vanilla extract, usually in the baking aisle. If you don't have any, you can always substitute with vanilla.*
- *To make this vegan, use a dairy-free yoghurt alternative.*

Blueberry, date and tahini smoothie

SERVES | **TIME TO MAKE** | **SUITABLE FOR**
4 | 🕐 **10 MINS** | GF VE

A great alternative to nut butter, tahini adds a smooth, creamy touch to this smoothie. If you don't like or don't have bananas, Medjool dates are a great sweet alternative. Blueberries give this delicious smoothie its deep purple colour and are packed with antioxidants.

6 Medjool dates, pitted
300g frozen blueberries
700ml coconut water
4 tbsp tahini
2 tbsp maple syrup

1. Put the dates in a small bowl and pour over enough boiling water to cover them. This will help them soften and plump up before blending.

2. Put the blueberries and coconut water into a blender and whizz until smooth. Drain the dates and add them to the blender with the tahini and maple syrup. Whizz again until smooth. Taste and adjust sweetness or add more liquid as needed.

Notes
· The mixture will keep in the fridge for up to 3 days.
· I've used coconut water here but any liquid, milk or milk alternative works well.

Fresh green smoothie

SERVES | **TIME TO MAKE** | **SUITABLE FOR**
4 | 🕐 **5 MINS** | VE GF

Vibrant green in colour, this smoothie uses frozen mango for sweetness and texture. Foods high in Vitamin C (such as orange) help absorb iron (spinach is a great source). Adding a pinch of salt to smoothies can seem a bit odd, but it really helps cut through any overly sweet flavours.

4 large handfuls of spinach
500ml coconut water
1 orange, peeled
500g frozen mango
2 tbsp almond butter
Juice of 2 limes
Pinch of salt

Add everything to a blender and blitz together until smooth.

Notes
· The smoothie will keep in the fridge for up to 3 days.
· I've used coconut water here but any liquid, milk or milk alternative works well.
· Use kale instead of spinach, but make sure you pull the leaves away from the tough stalk. This gives the smoothie an even deeper green colour.
· Use pineapple as an alternative to mango.

Warm coconut and chocolate malt smoothie

SERVES 4 | **TIME TO MAKE** 10 MINS | **SUITABLE FOR** VE GF

This thick, rich smoothie can be enjoyed cold, but there's something special about warming it up on a cold morning when you're short on time and fancy a smoothie but the thought of chugging back something ice-cold gives you brain freeze. An energising and comforting hug in a mug with a blend of coconut, chocolate and malty flavours.

100g fresh coconut flesh
600ml coconut milk
4 tbsp cocoa powder, plus extra to finish
4 tbsp rice malt syrup
2 tsp vanilla bean paste (or use vanilla extract)
80g rolled oats
4 tbsp desiccated coconut, to finish

1. Put all of the ingredients, except the desiccated coconut, in a blender and whizz until smooth.

2. Pour the mixture into a saucepan and place over a medium heat to warm through, stirring often. Do not bring to the boil. Remove from the heat and pour into mugs. Top each mug with a tablespoon of desiccated coconut and a pinch of cocoa powder.

Notes
· The blended mixture will keep for up to 3 days in the fridge.
· Fresh coconut is found in most supermarkets, in the fruit and vegetable aisle, often pre-chopped in snack pots.
· You can use maple syrup instead of rice malt syrup.
· If you're a coffee lover (like me), chocolate and coffee make one of the best combinations – add a shot of espresso and reduce the amount of coconut milk.
· If your saucepan doesn't have a 'lip', pour the warmed smoothie into a measuring jug and then into mugs for less splashing and spillage.

Cherry Negroni

SERVES | TIME TO MAKE | SUITABLE FOR
4 | 5 MINS | VE GF

It's not often I mess with the classics. Designed to be sipped slowly, a Negroni is hands-down one of my favourite celebratory cocktails. Equal parts gin, Campari and sweet red vermouth – it's a strong, smooth and slightly bitter cocktail, which is balanced by the vermouth and sweet orange twist garnish. This drink was inspired by the Cherry Blossom Negroni from the incredible, modern Chinese fusion restaurant Tattu, so if you can get your hands on cherry-blossom-flavoured vermouth, do give it a try. Otherwise, if you're curious for a sweet and tart lift to the classic, here's my twist.

Ice
160ml gin
160ml Campari
160ml sweet vermouth
160ml tart cherry juice
Orange twist and fresh cherries, to garnish

1. Add ice to 4 short tumbler glasses.

2. Pour the gin, Campari, sweet vermouth and cherry juice into a jug with a generous amount of ice. Stir vigorously for about 30 seconds until the outside of the glass feels cold. Strain and pour immediately into the glasses. Garnish with an orange twist and a fresh cherry.

Note
· This is one of my favourite cocktails to pre-mix into jam jars for a sunset picnic, BYO movie or dinner date.

Port and tonic (the new G&T)

SERVES | TIME TO MAKE | SUITABLE FOR
4 | 5 MINS | VE GF

P&Ts are the new G&Ts. Incredibly refreshing and deliciously different, 'Porto Tonico' is a well-loved drink in Portugal but rarely seen elsewhere. I was first served this on a very hot summer's day in Devon, with wildflowers blowing and people relaxing outside enjoying the weather; it was a recommendation from the bartender and it soon became my summer go-to! White port sales saw an 11 per cent increase over the last year, and white port can be found in most major supermarkets.

240ml white port
Handful of ice
480ml tonic water
Orange wedges, mint leaves and sprigs of thyme, to garnish

1. Pour the measured port between 4 tall glasses and add some ice cubes to each.

2. Top with cold tonic water and garnish with orange wedges, mint leaves and a few sprigs of thyme.

Note
· Try some other brilliant combinations to garnish: blackberry and basil leaves, lemon and rosemary and lime and mint leaves all work beautifully.

Homemade limoncello

SERVES | TIME TO MAKE | SUITABLE FOR
4 | 30 MINS | VE GF

10 unwaxed organic lemons
750ml vodka
800g caster sugar
800ml boiling water

Notes
- *Organic lemons are important here as non-organic are often coated with wax.*
- *Because every batch is different, I tend to add half the sugar syrup to the steeped vodka and lemon peel mixture and then taste before I add any more, adding the syrup gradually until I'm happy with the flavour. The more you add, the more diluted, more sweet and less intensely 'lemony' your limoncello will be.*

Often served as a digestif (or even aperitif) with dinner in Italy, this bright, intensely refreshing drink balances lemon's sweet, citrus and tart flavours and is always served chilled, usually in a shot glass. Incredibly simple and satisfying to make your own at home, this makes a wonderful gift to bring to a dinner party. Use the highest proof vodka you can find and let the peels and alcohol mingle for at least a week and up to 1 month. The longer you leave it the stronger the flavour will be.

1. Use a vegetable peeler to peel all the rind from the lemons, trying not to get any of the bitter white pith with it – trim any away with a knife. Put the zest ribbons into a large, sterilised jar (I use a 5-litre one) and pour over the vodka. Cover tightly and leave for at least 1 week, gently shaking the jar each day. Store away from direct light. Most of the work is done in the first week, though the longer you leave it the stronger it will be. The lemon peels will lose their colour over the week, which is what we want to see.

2. Make the simple sugar syrup by pouring the water into a large saucepan over a medium heat. Add the sugar and whisk with a balloon whisk at a gentle simmer until all of the sugar has dissolved, about 2 minutes. Leave this to cool and then use a funnel to pour this sugar mixture into the large jar with the vodka and lemon peel.

3. Line a sieve with a clean muslin cloth, cheesecloth or coffee filter and strain the limoncello into a large, clean jar or measuring jug. Use a funnel to then pour the strained mixture into one or several smaller sterilised glass bottles with tight-fitting lids

4. Keep in the fridge for 1 month or in the freezer for up to 1 year. Label with the bottling date and always serve chilled.

Bloody Mary

SERVES | TIME TO MAKE | SUITABLE FOR
4 | 10 MINS | VE GF

So much more than just tomato juice and a shot of vodka. Layers of spice add lots of flavour, heat and sweetness, making this a drink you can sip and really enjoy rather than throw back on a hangover and hope for the best. One of the things I love most about the bloody Mary is the garnishes – go for anything bright green and fresh-looking to make it visually come to life.

1 litre tomato juice
1 small cucumber, peeled and deseeded
1 tbsp prepared horseradish
½ tsp smoked paprika
Pinch of salt
6 dashes of Worcestershire sauce
6 dashes of Tabasco/hot sauce
Freshly ground black pepper
Juice of 1 lemon
Juice of 1 lime
200ml vodka

TO GARNISH
Parsley sprigs, green olives, celery sticks, cucumber ribbons
Lemon or lime wedge and salt or celery salt (for the glass rims)

1. Put all the ingredients except the vodka into a blender and whizz until smooth. Taste and adjust the seasoning to your own preference.

2. Rub the rims of 4 tall highball glasses with a lemon or lime wedge, then roll them in the salt or celery salt until fully coated. Fill your glasses with ice.

3. Pour 50ml vodka into each glass, then top with the bloody Mary mix and stir with a celery stick (or spoon). Garnish with whatever takes your fancy and serve.

Notes
· You can also serve this in one large jug and let your guests just help themselves.
· Just as with the margarita mix, you can skip the vodka and serve as a morning-after treat.
· The blended mixture will keep for up to 5 days in the fridge.

Homemade margarita mix

SERVES | **TIME TO MAKE** | **SUITABLE FOR**
4 | 🕐 **30 MINS** | **VE** **GF**

Just add tequila! Much fresher and tastier than shop-bought mixers, this makes a wonderful gift or something to bring to a party. Just add tequila, triple sec, ice and a slice and you're good to go. It's also great for making large pitchers and if you'd like your margaritas frozen, just throw in a few handfuls of ice and blend in a smoothie maker. Salted rims not only make the cocktails look amazing but the purpose of the salt is to cut through any bitterness and balance out the acidity from the lime.

FOR THE MARGARITA MIX
200g caster sugar
Zest of 5 limes and juice of 10
½ tsp salt

FOR THE CHILLI LIME SALT
1 tbsp chilli powder
4 tbsp salt
Zest of 1 lime

TO SERVE
Lime wedges, to garnish
200ml tequila
100ml triple sec

1. Start by making a simple sugar syrup. Heat the sugar and 250ml water in a saucepan over a low heat until the sugar has dissolved. Remove from the heat and let the mixture cool.

2. Once the sugar syrup has cooled, pour in the lime zest and juice and salt, mixing together well. Use a clean funnel to pour this into a bottle. Refrigerate the mix for up to 2 weeks.

3. For the chilli lime salt, mix everything together.

4. To assemble your margaritas, pour the chilli lime salt into a shallow plate. Rub a wedge of lime around the rim of each margarita glass and dip and twist into the salt mixture. Fill the glasses with ice and add 50ml tequila and 25ml triple sec to each glass. Top up with the margarita mix, stir vigorously and serve with a lime wedge on the side.

Notes
· Swap the lime juice for grapefruit or orange juice.
· My perfect margarita ratio is 75ml margarita mix, 50ml tequila, 25ml triple sec.

Rum-spiked hot chocolate

SERVES | TIME TO MAKE | SUITABLE FOR

2 | **10** MINS | **V**

Not just for Christmas, this velvety and smooth mix is perfect for any cool evening. I first had it camping in the National Park of Australia's beautiful Jervis Bay, surrounded by free-roaming kangaroos, next to a campfire underneath the stars.

250ml any milk
60g dark chocolate (70% cocoa solids), finely chopped
2 tsp cocoa powder
½ tsp ground cinnamon (optional)
1 tbsp soft light brown sugar
Pinch of salt
30ml rum
Marshmallows, to top

1. Add the milk to a small saucepan and place over a medium heat until it comes to a gentle simmer, then reduce to a low heat and add the chopped chocolate. Slowly melt together, occasionally using a balloon whisk to mix. Once melted, add the cocoa powder, cinnamon (if using), sugar and salt, whisking to mix.

2. Remove from the heat and add the rum, stirring well.

3. Pour into a thick-rimmed glass or mug and pile with marshmallows.

Notes
· Swap the rum for brandy, Irish liqueur or leave out the alcohol altogether.
· Add a tablespoon of almond or nut butter for a delicious nutty flavour.
· To make this vegan, use a dairy-free milk alternative.

Index

HarperCollins*Publishers*
1 London Bridge Street
London SE1 9GF

www.harpercollins.co.uk

HarperCollins*Publishers*
1st Floor, Watermarque Building,
Ringsend Road
Dublin 4, Ireland

First published by HarperCollins*Publishers* 2022

10 9 8 7 6 5 4 3 2 1

Text © Lucy Lord 2022

Photography by Martin Poole
© HarperCollins*Publishers* 2022

Lucy Lord asserts the moral right
to be identified as the author of this work

A catalogue record of this book is
available from the British Library

ISBN 978-0-00-852114-1

Food styling by Pippa Leon
Prop styling by Max Robinson

Printed and bound in Latvia

MIX
Paper from
responsible sources
FSC™ C007454

FSC
www.fsc.org

This book is produced from independently certified FSC™ paper
to ensure responsible forest management.

For more information visit: www.harpercollins.co.uk/green

Acknowledgements

So much time, dedication, creativity and talent
has gone in to bringing *Cook for the Soul* to
life, many of those who you don't see between
these pages.

From the food styling, the colour palettes,
the props, the backdrops – thank you Pippa,
Jojo, Simone and Max for bringing my recipes
to life. Thank you to Martin Poole for your
passion and approach in capturing these
beautiful images and Grace for your attention
to detail. It really was a dream come true to
work with you all.

A huge thank you to everyone at
HarperCollins who has helped bring this book
to life. Sarah, Lydia and James. Thank you so
much for your time, hard work and creativity.
Thank you for caring about it as much as I do.

Thank you Tony for your generosity and
the best kitchen I could have ever worked
from. Thank you all the Markeys for your
kindness – the brownies are dedicated to you!

Thank you to Luke for your friendship,
relentless work and support. Thank you P and
the many friends who have helped sample
kitchen experiments – especially on the days
where everything went wrong! Thank you,
Steph, for everything.

Finally, my deepest gratitude to you, the
reader. Thank you for joining my journey,
supporting my passions and allowing me to
continue to live this dream of creating new
recipes with purpose. I will never take it
for granted.

Create, share, make a mess and then start
all over again – it's good for the soul.